NEGOTIATION IN INTERNATIONAL CONFLICT

THE SANDHURST CONFERENCE SERIES
ISSN 1468-1153
Series Editor: Matthew Midlane

NEGOTIATION IN INTERNATIONAL CONFLICT

Understanding Persuasion

Edited by
DEBORAH GOODWIN
Royal Military Academy Sandhurst

THE SANDHURST CONFERENCE SERIES

General Editor
Matthew Midlane

FRANK CASS
LONDON • PORTLAND, OR

First Published in 2002 in Great Britain by
FRANK CASS & CO. LTD.
Crown House, 47 Chase Side
Southgate, London N14 5BP

and in the United States of America by
FRANK CASS
c/o ISBS, 5804 N.E. Hassalo Street
Portland, Oregon 97213-3644

British Library Cataloguing in Publication Data:

Negotiation in international conflict: understanding
persuasion. – (The Sandhurst Conference series; no. 4)
1. Negotiation 2. Pacific settlement of international
disputes 3. Intervention (International law) 4. Peacekeeping
forces
I. Goodwin, Deborah II. Royal Military Academy
302.3'024355

ISBN 0 7146 5191 5 (cloth)
ISBN 0 7146 8193 8 (paper)

Library of Congress Cataloging-in-Publication Data:

Negotiation in international conflict: understanding persuasion /
edited by Deborah Goodwin.
    p.   cm. – (The Sandhurst conference series; 4)
  Includes bibliographical references and index.
  ISBN 0 7146 5191 5 (cloth) – ISBN 0 7146 8193 8 (pbk.)
  1. International police. 2. Negotiation. 3. Conflict
management. I. Goodwin, Deborah. II. Series.
JZ6374 .N44 2001
327.1'7–dc21

2001032459

Typeset in 10.5/12.5pt Classical Garamond by Vitaset, Paddock Wood, Kent
Printed in Great Britain by Creative Print and Design, Wales, Ebbw Vale

Contents

Figures

For all the peacekeepers around the world,
and my family.

Contributors

ROBIN BROWN Robin Brown's research interests concern aspects of communications policy and the political effects of new communications technology. He is based at the Institute of Communication Studies, University of Leeds. He has published *Globalization and the State* (Cambridge: Polity Press, 1997) and *From Cold War to Collapse: Theory and World Politics in the 1980s* (Cambridge: Cambridge University Press, 1992). He lectures in political communications and communication policy issues. His chapter is based on the paper delivered at the Sandhurst conference on negotiation held in March 1999.

SUSAN C. DRISCOLL is a psychologist working with the Defence Evaluation Research Agency. Her interests concern semiotics and images as represented in the media and in interpersonal encounters.

DEBORAH GOODWIN is a senior lecturer in the Department of Communication Studies, Royal Military Academy Sandhurst. She has lectured both in the UK and internationally on many aspects of negotiation, and her PhD research covers low-level military negotiation tactics and structure. In March 1999 she organised a conference on negotiation at Sandhurst, which formed the inspiration for this publication. In October 1999 she conducted training on negotiation for delegates from around the world attending the international peacekeeping negotiation and mediation course at the Pearson Peacekeeping Centre, Canada. She also lectures widely within the UK on this subject, and has worked with the US War College, and Fort Bragg.

STUART GORDON is a senior lecturer in Defence and International Affairs, Royal Military Academy Sandhurst. He has numerous publications to his name and his specialism lies in mediative dispute resolution at the strategic and operational levels of a conflict.

STEPHEN HILL is an assistant professor in the Political Science Department at the University of Georgia, in Athens, Georgia. Previous publications include a co-authored text, *Peacekeeping and the United Nations* (Dartmouth Press, 1996), 'Disarmament in Mozambique: Learning the Lessons of Experience', *Contemporary Security Policy*, 17: 1 (1996), and 'To Prosecute or Not', *The World Today*, 56: 8 (2000).

ALEXANDER KENNAWAY worked at the Conflict Studies Research Centre based at RMA Sandhurst. A Russian by birth, he moved to Britain and served with the Royal Navy before embarking on an academic career. He was a prolific writer and speaker, and died in May 2000, prior to the publication of this book. His widow has kindly given permission for his work to be included here.

BRAD McRAE holds a doctoral degree in counselling psychology from the University of British Columbia, and is a psychologist, consultant and the president of McRae & Associates, his company which provides services in staff training and development and management consulting. He was trained in negotiation skills at the Project on Negotiation at Harvard University, and lectures on negotiation across Canada and the United States. He has written the following books: *Negotiating and Influencing Skills: The Art of Creating and Claiming Value*; *How to Write a Thesis and Keep your Sanity*; and *Practical Time Management: How to get More Done in Less Time*.

ASHLEY STOCKER is a staff officer for the British Army Civil Affairs Group based at Gibraltar Barracks, Minley. The group is responsible for developing liaison with civilian agencies such as international organisations (UN, Oxfam, etc.), governmental organisations (DFID, USAID) and non-governmental organisations (Oxfam, MSF), and local government and civilian agencies when the military deploy on operations.

KEITH WEBB is the director of studies of the International Conflict Analysis Programme at the Graduate School of International Relations, University of Kent, Canterbury. He has been involved in political-level mediation in Moldova, and is currently assisting in the production of the Moldovan constitution.

Series Editor's Preface

Negotiation in International Conflict: Understanding Persuasion is the third volume in the Sandhurst Conference Series, following *The Media and International Security* edited by Stephen Badsey and *Aspects of Peacekeeping* edited by D.S. Gordon and F.H. Toase. They will be followed by *Britain, NATO and the Lessons of the Balkan Conflict*, edited by Stephen Badsey and Paul Latawski. All the titles draw their inspiration from a series of international conferences held at the Royal Military Academy Sandhurst in recent years. Their purpose has been to draw together the diverse communities of academia, the military, the civil service and the media to explore issues which have arisen or become more salient in the post-Cold War era. Discussion has been intense, at times fierce, but in practice there has been more common ground than had seemed likely when we planned the conference. That said, they provide an enormously valuable forum in which to explore differences and edge towards a sense of mutual understanding.

This volume has its origins in the research of the editor, Deborah Goodwin, who has pioneered work on negotiation skills in the Department of Communication Studies at Sandhurst, which has introduced the subject to the academy's syllabus. At Sandhurst the debate has drawn military and academic colleagues ever closer as we seek ways to improve the training and education of our aspirant officers. *Negotiation in International Conflict* is a discussion of negotiation at all levels of command, from the strategic to the tactical, but with its main emphasis on the importance of developing this skill in more junior commanders. It has a theoretical backdrop but keeps firmly in the foreground the need to formulate clear guidelines on the practical art of negotiation in the field as well as in the cabinet room. For many it will be an introductory volume to a subject of which they are generally aware but have no detailed knowledge. Few issues could be of more direct relevance to the British Army, which has been immersed in Peace Support Operations for the last decade.

Matthew Midlane,
Royal Military Academy Sandhurst

Foreword

MAJOR-GENERAL A.G. DENARO CBE

Having been involved over many years in the training of negotiation techniques, and now as Commandant at Sandhurst being responsible for the education and training of young officers as they go out to command in the difficult and dangerous circumstances that prevail today, it has been interesting to reflect on the essays contained in this excellent volume. A soldier is likely to be involved at both ends of the spectrum, from the early discussions with possible adversaries, to the final conflict-resolution, if force is necessary. He must of course be well trained for the latter as the final deterrent, but his ability in the hugely complex business of the former is becoming more and more necessary.

Recent deployments have shown the greater emphasis towards conciliation and consent in 'operations other than war'. The importance of diplomacy in negotiation at every level of command is an essential tool and will become clear in the discussions and analysis presented in this volume.

What is also becoming clear is how good the soldier and young officer actually is at this business. We are witnessing the re-emergence of the historic concept of the soldier diplomat. Around the world armed forces are reviewing and rebuilding basic training programmes in order to educate the modern interventionist in the critical business of relating to people and clear communication. The act of persuading people that it is better to live peacefully than to survive in a state of war, that it is more effective to work together towards a common good than to kill each other, is only really effective at the grassroots level, which is where our soldiers operate. Many fine words may be spoken in the corridors of power, but unless those protagonists involved on the ground can see improvements occurring and are really persuaded of them, they will never agree to lay down their arms. The operational techniques of negotiation, mediation and the use of civil affairs teams are critically important today and remain an absolute requirement of an effective war-fighter.

A.G. Denaro,
October 2000

Introduction

This book is an exploration of the increasing importance of negotiation as a dispute-resolution technique at all levels of a conflict. Whilst there has been some analysis of the role and impact of negotiation at the political and strategic levels of a situation, to date there has been little investigation of the nature of *tactical level* negotiation and the way in which this duty is impacting upon the responsibilities of the serving soldier. This wide range of negotiated agreements by a multiplicity of parties infers that the nature of negotiation itself must be different at various levels of command. In other words, negotiation is being used to achieve different ends, and ought to be viewed as a multifaceted skill which contains a variety of impetuses and desired outcomes. It may be argued that the type of negotiation in which Richard Holbrooke is involved (in Bosnia-Herzegovina) at the political/strategic level will have different ramifications from those of the soldier on the ground negotiating his way through an illegal checkpoint, for example.

The chapters in this book originate from the Negotiation and Mediation Conference held at the Royal Military Academy Sandhurst in March 1999. Several of the contributors spoke at this conference, and other informed individuals in this field of research have added their contributions to the book.

Part 1 of this book looks at the role and nature of negotiation on the world stage. Part 2 seeks to begin the discussion on the tactical-level aspects of negotiation, and the way in which the modern soldier is having to adapt to new rules of engagement, especially in peacekeeping operations. Modern mandates often require the protagonist to use negotiation as a first resort and armed force as the last; we shall discuss the implications of this for the peacekeeper. Part 3 focuses on particular case-studies: the making of a new constitution in Moldova; the role of negotiation in the deployment of UNPROFOR in Bosnia from 1992–95; and the nature and culture of Russians and their approach to interpersonal skills.

It is to our great regret that Alexander Kennaway, author of Chapter 10, died before this book went to the printers. His chapter is one of his last pieces, and I am very pleased to include it here.

Deborah Goodwin

Acknowledgements

The editor wishes to thank the following: Matthew Midlane, Director of Studies RMAS for his support; John Allen, Head of the Communication Studies Department, RMAS for his encouragement in the development of negotiation training in the Communication Studies Department RMAS; Sarah Oliver at the Central Library RMAS for her unstinting assistance in finding material; and Betty Barton for her help in typing sections of the manuscript.

The views expressed in this book are those of the authors and in no way reflect the views of the Ministry of Defence.

Abbreviations and Glossary

ANC	African National Congress.
BATNA	best alternative to a negotiated agreement.
B-H	Bosnia-Herzegovina.
CA	Civil Affairs.
CCA	Centre for Conflict Analysis.
CIS	Commonwealth of Independent States (Russia and satellite states – old Soviet Union).
DFID	Department for International Development.
EC	European Community.
ECHO	European Communities Humanitarian Office.
EU	European Union.
FCO	Foreign and Commonwealth Office.
FIS	Foundation for International Security.
GPA	general peace agreement.
HQ	headquarters.
ICRC	International Committee of the Red Cross.
IFOR	Implementation Force.
IRA	Irish Republican Army.
LO	liaison officer.
MAI	Multilateral Agreement on Investment.
MSF	Médecins sans Frontières.
NATO	North Atlantic Treaty Organisation.
NGO	non-governmental organisation.
ODA	Overseas Development Agency.
OECD	Organisation for Economic Cooperation and Development.
OSCE	Organisation for Security and Cooperation in Europe.
PLO	Palestine Liberation Organisation.
PSW	problem-solving workshop.

Psyops   Psychological Operations.
ROEs   rules of engagement.
SOPs   standard operating procedures.
UNFICKP   United Nations Peacekeeping Force in Cyprus.
UNHCR   United Nations High Commission for Refugees.
UNITAF   United Task Force (Somalia, 1992).
UNOSOM (I and II)   United Nations Operation in Somalia.
UNPROFOR   United Nations Protection Force (March 1992–
                    September 1993). UN force in the Balkans.
USAID   United States Agency for International Development.
USSR   Union of Soviet Socialist Republics (Soviet Union).

PART 1
The Place of Negotiation in the World Today

Negotiating within Cultures: The United Nations and the Resolution of Civil Conflict

STEPHEN HILL

INTRODUCTION

At the beginning of the 1980s few people could have predicted the dramatic changes which were to take place within the international political system by the end of the decade. The election of Mikhail Gorbachev as General Secretary of the USSR in 1985 heralded an end to over four decades of ideological confrontation and effectively eradicated the risk of military conflict. Spurred on by domestic financial pressures, both superpowers sought peace dividends by ending overtly expensive support for regimes in areas of the world which they no longer deemed to be in their national interest. The international community, caught up in the euphoria brought about by the expectation of a new peaceful age, hoped that all that would be required was a method of overseeing the conclusion of conflicts which had resulted from, and been sustained by, a now defunct global rivalry.

However, expectations that the proxy wars fought on behalf of the superpowers would dry up, along with the financial and military support they provided, were to be sadly misguided. Rather, the retreat of superpower hegemony simply uncovered a Pandora's box of cultural, ethnic, religious and nationalistic disagreements, which were all too ready to fill the vacuum left behind and which possessed a force and momentum of their own. With the fog of Cold War antagonism lifting, public attention focused on the ability of the major international powers to resolve these conflicts, which through war and famine were claiming hundreds of thousands of victims every year. With a consensus never before attained, the international community turned to the UN, not only to oversee the withdrawal of the superpowers themselves but to attempt ever increasingly ambitious methods of bringing seemingly intractable conflicts to a peaceful conclusion.

The dilemma facing the UN in its attempts to reconcile warring parties and reconstruct these so called 'failed states' was apparent. As Licklider writes:

> Ending international war is hard enough, but at least there the opponents will presumably eventually retreat to their own territories ... But in civil wars the members of the two sides must live side by side and work together in a common government to make the country work ... How do groups of people who have been killing one another with considerable enthusiasm and success come together to form a common government.[1]

As if this dilemma were not enough to deal with, the UN's peacemaking efforts were to be complicated by a new dimension presented by such intrastate conflicts: the need to negotiate with non-state actors. As Sydney Bailey noted, 'the [UN] Charter was drafted on the assumption that disputes arise between states and included no provision by which the Security Council or General Assembly [could] relate to non-state agencies such as liberation movements, communal minorities, or political parties'.[2] In the early post-Cold War operations the UN avoided such complications by omitting non-state actors from settlement negotiations. This was the case for the various mujahadeen in Afghanistan and the resistance factions in Angola and Namibia.[3] However, the nature of the conflicts in which the UN was later to become involved prescribed that the organisation had little choice but to include such non-state actors in negotiations. In fact by the time the UN became involved in the humanitarian tragedy in Somalia in 1992, the only actors left to deal with were those of a non-state type.

As this chapter will show, the UN's increasing involvement in the resolution of civil wars has forced it to come to terms with the particular problems posed by negotiations with non-state actors in non-western cultures. As the UN was eventually to realise, the various non-state entities with which it was now being called to negotiate were mostly unaffected by the expectations of the Western-orientated 'diplomatic culture' which pervaded the formal circles of interstate negotiations.[4] The initial failure of the UN to take account of this not only led it to expect behaviour incongruous with the cultural traditions of the internal parties themselves but also allowed the UN to attempt conflict-resolution procedures incompatible with the cultures within which they were being introduced. The UN's cultural sensitivity, or lack of it, goes a long way to explaining the relative success or failure of many of its past peacekeeping missions.

In order to show how and why this has been the case, this chapter will compare the UN's experiences in four of its peacekeeping operations conducted between 1991 and 1995. These include the second Angolan mission (1991–92), together with the operations in Cambodia (1991–93), Mozambique (1992–94) and Somalia (1992–95).[5]

The objective of this chapter is threefold. First, to show how the frustrations felt by the UN when internal parties failed to 'honour' negotiated agreements was to a significant extent created by its own cultural misunderstandings. Second, to illustrate that although the UN managed to develop cultural sensitivity in at least one of its operations in order to avert a mission failure, in others the organisation still retained the potential to be culturally insensitive. Third, and finally, to show how the eventual outcomes of peacekeeping operations can be affected by the UN's sensitivity (or lack of it) to the cultural contexts in which it operates.

ANGOLA

With the signing of the Accords de Paz para Angola on 31 May 1991, the two main parties to the civil war, the Movimento Popular de Lieragao de Angola (MPLA) and Uniao Nacional para a Independencia Total de Angola (UNITA), agreed to disband their respective armies, create a new unified armed force and conduct democratic elections within 17 months. Initially, the UN was to be given only a peripheral role in the peace process. Essentially the organisation's role was to monitor the workings of the body created to oversee the implementation of the accords, the Joint Political Military Commission (CCPM), which was to be composed of members of both parties. However, a combination of a lack of preparation and inadequate resources ensured that the UN was to be dragged further and further into helping the parties fulfil their obligations. By the time the elections were held, the UN had become the official electoral observer and was increasingly involved in providing help for the demobilisation of the parties' forces and the creation of the national force.[6]

Despite the UN's efforts, however, the Angolan operation was to end in disaster. UNITA's leader Jonas Savimbi refused to accept the election results, which not only placed his party second in the parliamentary elections but more importantly placed him second in the presidential elections. The results, declared free and fair on 11 October 1992, gave the MPLA and UNITA 53.7 per cent and 34.1 per cent respectively in the parliamentary elections. The MPLA candidate, Jose Eduardo dos Santos, won 49.57 per cent, whilst Savimbi won 40.07 per cent in the presidential elections. Although the failure of either presidential candidate to win over 50 per cent of the votes meant that a run-off election was required within six weeks, Savimbi refused to wait and UNITA returned to war. Angola was once again plunged into chaos.

The 17-month period of the Angolan operation was a source of constant frustration for the UN and its negotiators. Despite their commitments to disarm and demobilise their forces before elections were held, neither party in fact did so. By June 1992, only three months before the elections, barely 4 per cent of UNITA's forces had demobilised and approximately 18 per cent of the MPLA's had done the same. Regardless of the UN's attempts to negotiate new commitments from both parties and the constant reaffirmations of the accords which it received from both leaders, neither party fulfilled its promises.

Expectations that the UN could negotiate the disarmament of either party in the circumstances prevailing in Angola were essentially grounded in a misunderstanding of the cultural context of the operation. The 'Western' state system, imposed by the colonial powers on traditional African cultures, has in many instances resulted in the power of the state becoming simply another resource for which to compete. The democratic process in such circumstances becomes a winner-take-all strategy, in which the concept of democratic opposition is anathema to so-called political parties mostly formed along ethnic, religious or tribal grounds. This cultural difference with regard to the organisation of the state was elaborated by Pondi, when at a conference held on the future of Angola he stated that

> The 'winner-take-all' strategy which is enforced in Western democratic society cannot be accepted in the context of Africa because the state is a distributive instrument rather than a productive one. It does not organise or galvanise people into productivity but is perceived as something over which one has control in order to distribute and to take control of the resources of the country.[7]

This cultural mindset was initially apparent during the negotiations for the accords. Despite the attempts of some of those present to persuade the parties to agree to an accommodation for the eventual losers of the elections, neither party would accept such a settlement. Indeed, 'each was bent on nothing less than total victory'.[8] UNITA had even called for elections to be held within 12 months of the start of the operation – an indication that it perceived democratic elections as little more than an opportunity for the peaceful transference of power.[9] In such a cultural context the UN could not hope to negotiate the disarmament of either party or the eventual peaceful transference of power. In fact the UN's willingness to continue negotiations whilst the parties repeatedly failed to fulfil their obligations has been blamed by some for giving UNITA the impression that compliance with the military elements of the accords was unimportant because it was destined to win power anyway.[10]

CAMBODIA

In contrast to the operation in Angola, the UN's involvement in the Cambodian peace process was intended to be far more intrusive. The Comprehensive Political Settlement of Cambodia, signed on 23 October 1991, required the UN not only to supervise the disarmament of the four main parties' forces but also to create a 'neutral political environment' conducive to free and fair elections. To achieve this all governmental administrative agencies, bodies and offices which could directly influence the outcome of elections were placed under direct UN supervision or control. The UN was also required to organise and conduct the elections – not just supervise them as it had done in Angola.

By May 1992, however, the operation was already beginning to falter. The Khmer Rouge, by far the largest of the three resistance factions, began to refuse to assemble and disarm its troops, blaming its intransigence on the failure of the UN to fulfil its promises to ensure either a neutral political environment or the withdrawal of Vietnamese forces. Although the UN claimed the Khmer Rouge had misinterpreted the agreements and the UN's role in their implementation, no amount of negotiations could persuade the Khmer Rouge to return to the peace process.

By November 1992, therefore, the UN Secretary-General, Boutros Boutros-Ghali, knowing that none of the parties had disarmed their troops, was faced with the decision of whether or not to continue to hold the elections planned for May 1993. Despite attempts by the Khmer Rouge to disrupt the elections with the threat of violence, the Secretary-General was able to declare the poll both 'free and fair' on 29 May 1993, although he could not say the same for the electoral campaign.[11] When the final results were released on 10 June the party of the nominal government, the Cambodian Peoples Party (CPP) had won only 38.23 per cent of the vote. One of the three resistance factions, the Front Uni National pour un Cambodge Indépendant, Neutre, Pacifique et Co-opératif (FUNCINPEC), led by the country's former head of state, Prince Sihanouk, had won 45.47 per cent of the vote.[12]

Unhappy and unwilling to accept the election result the CPP candidates of the new assembly resigned in protest, claiming electoral fraud. In order to prevent a military coup by the CPP, which still controlled the army and the main organs of government, Prince Sihanouk established a 50–50 power-sharing arrangement between the CPP and FUNCINPEC. Although the UN initially refused to accept such an undemocratic outcome, the unpredictable circumstances of post-electoral Cambodia ensured its eventual acquiescence. The CPP had, therefore, managed to threaten its way back into power.[13]

As in Angola, the UN's negotiations with the internal parties were to take place in a cultural context which it did not fully appreciate. Its hopes to negotiate a return of the Khmer Rouge and of the peaceful transference of power following democratic elections were both forlorn. This argument is posited by Pierre Lizee, who has suggested that the refusal of the Cambodian parties to participate in the peace process as the UN had expected was based on their idiosyncratic cultural attitudes towards conflict and democracy. Whilst the UN's 'Western' traditions prescribed 'liberal democracy' through the organisation of elections as the key to the transformation of the conflict, Cambodian society, dominated by Brahmanism and Buddhism, confined social interactions to small groups of personal relations in which 'well-defined status and ranks' and predestined 'fatalistic outlooks' precluded its introduction. When the French, during their period of colonial rule, introduced legal and administrative structures into the Cambodian state, they did so by superimposing them over the traditional cultural influences of Cambodian society. The Western model of the state and the requisite understanding of democracy had just never properly developed.[14] Indeed, until a few years ago, the words 'society' and 'consensus' did not even exist in Khmer language.[15]

Throughout their negotiations with the UN the common denominator between all the internal factions was their refusal to move politics beyond the factionalism which characterised Cambodian society.[16] The failure to appreciate the Cambodian understanding of conflict, articulated as it is around the 'family-patronage–dynastic' (Buddhist) model, led the UN into inappropriate negotiating strategies. This was never more evident than when the UN promulgated its first electoral law in April 1992, which by allowing 'every Cambodian person ... over the age of 18 ... to be registered as a voter', challenged the local notion that political and civil rights are derived from Khmer custom and culture. Despite attempts to rewrite the electoral law the UN continued to base enfranchisement on where the person, their parents, or grandparents were born, and not on their ethnic grouping – something which all parties in the Cambodian peace process found unacceptable.[17]

MOZAMBIQUE

It could have been construed as ominous that the signing of the General Peace Agreement (GPA) on 15 October 1992 took place at a time when the Angolan operation was in a state of collapse and the Cambodia mission was experiencing similar difficulties. However, in light of the lessons learned through its experiences in Angola, the UN began to plan for a much greater role for itself in Mozambique.[18] Although its mandate was not to be as extensive as the one it had adopted in Cambodia, it was still to have a central role in the supervision of the implementation of the GPA, including the disarmament of the parties' forces, the creation of a new national force and the coordination of all humanitarian assistance operations. Nevertheless, the GPA still contained the excessively optimistic hope that democratic elections could be held within 12 months of the operation's beginning.

It came as no great surprise, therefore, when the failure of the parties to disarm their forces forced the UN to postpone the elections by one year, until October 1994. In a virtual re-enactment of the tragedy in Angola, the resistance faction in Mozambique, Resistencia Nacional Mozambicana (RENAMO), announced two days prior to polling that it was to withdraw from the elections, accusing the nominal government party, Frente da Libertacao de Mozambique (FRELIMO), of fraud. At the same time both internal parties retained substantial military capabilities outside of the disarmament process. Nevertheless, RENAMO returned to compete in the elections, winning 37.8 per cent of the vote against FRELIMO's 44.3 per cent in the legislative elections. RENAMO's leader, Afonso Dhlakama, and FRELIMO's leader, Joaquim Chissano, won 33.7 and 53.3 per cent of the vote respectively in the presidential elections.

It would seem, therefore, that the stage was set for another return to war in an African country in which democratic elections were incompatible with the culture in which they were being transplanted. However, the refusal of RENAMO to return to war was a direct result of the cultural sensitivity shown by the UN in its negotiations with RENAMO.

First, the UN acknowledged that RENAMO was ill-prepared to compete in democratic elections, accepting that it was simply not organised in the manner implied by the Western concept of 'political parties'. This was made clear in 1991 when RENAMO's political status was questioned during an insurance claim in the Commercial Court in London. Forced to rule on whether RENAMO held political objectives or was simply the foreign creation of Rhodesia and South Africa, Mr Justice Saville explained in his decision that the normal criteria used to distinguish political parties would not suffice in this case, because

9

The idea that any genuine political movement would necessarily have to prepare and publish carefully formulated programmes or manifestos for future government and seek to disseminate these views in the country is a peculiarly Western concept which to my mind cannot simply be applied to an organisation such as RENAMO operating in a country such as Mozambique.[19]

Indeed, apart from its call for democratic elections and a market economy, serious questions were asked as to whether RENAMO had any independent political platform at all.[20] Rather than continue with the operation regardless – the mistake it had made in Angola – the UN took the decision not only to postpone the elections for 12 months, but also to establish a trust fund to provide the resources required to help RENAMO transform into a political party capable of competing in democratic elections.

Second, in November 1993 the UN called for the creation of a 'more flexible instrument [than the trust fund] through which to channel about $300,000 per month' to Dhlakama until the elections. In his letter to the Italian government requesting that it make an initial contribution to the fund, the Secretary-General explained that '[if] the RENAMO leader is not enabled to meet the expectations of his supporters, he will lose the authority and prestige, and the entire peace process will be destabilised'.[21] Ajello reiterated the Secretary-General's assessment, stating that 'Dhlakama is regarded as an African chief ... and he needs to be able to act like one. He needs money to pension off his generals, to distribute largesse.'[22] By offering Dhlakama and his party over $11 million (part of which bought him a bullet-proof Mercedes and a beautiful house overlooking the Indian Ocean), the RENAMO leader was offered a means of saving face and a far better alternative than a return to the bush.[23] Ajello expressed the importance of the trust fund in this regard, describing it just before the elections as a 'most valuable instrument' with which 'Dhlakama [had] accepted giving up the military option and saw his vital interest in RENAMO's transformation into a political party.'[24] Dhlakama's description of himself in the wake of the elections illuminates this delicate balance between democracy and status: 'I am the second most important man in Mozambique and I am leader of the opposition.'[25]

Thus the cultural sensitivity of the UN enabled it to avert what could easily have been another Angolan catastrophe. It became apparent to the UN during 1993 that negotiations with RENAMO, which were continually failing to reap the objectives the organisation desired, were taking place in a cultural context which determined the internal parties' actions. Only by accepting and working within this cultural context could the UN negotiations succeed. However, as the next section covering the UN's involvement in Somalia will illustrate, the organisation still retained the capability to be culturally insensitive in other contexts.

SOMALIA

Unlike the other operations covered by this chapter the UN's involvement in Somalia did not arise as part of a comprehensive peace agreement reached between the internal parties. Rather, it evolved as a reaction to the need to protect the delivery of humanitarian relief. The UN was also to become involved in Somalia through not one but two operations: the UN Operation in Somalia (UNOSOM) and UNOSOM II, which it conducted through April 1992 and March 1995. During this period another operation was conducted, but this third operation consisted of a multinational coalition mandated by the UN Security Council and led by the United States: the Unified Task Force (UNITAF). This third operation was established in January 1992 and was replaced by UNOSOM II in May 1993.

Despite the eventual deployment of over 50,000 troops, and an expenditure in excess of $2 billion, the Somalian intervention eventually ended in disaster. As the UN and UNITAF struggled to restore order to a society which had reverted to a state of anarchy, they were to become increasingly involved in conflict with the local populace. Commensurate with its rising levels of irritation at the failure of local warlords to abide by negotiated agreements, the UN began to employ ever greater levels of coercion. This trend was to culminate in a number of pitched battles in which approximately 50 peacekeepers and thousands of Somalis were to lose their lives. In the face of such loss of life, popular support for the Somalian intervention began to crumble among contributing countries, leading to the announcement by President Clinton on 7 October 1993 of a complete withdrawal of US forces by the following March. Although UNOSOM II continued to operate after this time, it did so with a drastically scaled-down mandate.

Although all three operations were to differ quite substantially in the nature of their mandates and levels of deployment, all of them were to exhibit similar cultural insensitivities in their negotiations with local parties. However, this was not initially to be the case. The Secretary-General's first special representative in Somalia, Mohammed Sahnoun, a former Algerian diplomat, had attempted to negotiate with the local warlords, but had done so with the active involvement of local community elders. Although Sahnoun believed such a strategy to be essential to the

11

ultimate success of the UN's peacebuilding efforts, his culturally sensitive approach to negotiations was far too protracted for an organisation in need of quick results. Such organisational needs ran contrary to the traditional Somali approach to negotiations, which dictates that they may take months and indeed be continually open to change.[26] When the UN announced the deployment of 3,500 troops in August 1992, without previously consulting with either Somali leaders or community elders, the credibility of Sahnoun's negotiations were fatally undermined and he was left with little option but to resign.[27]

The UN's tendency to negotiate with the warlords directly, ignoring the importance of local elders, led in many cases to an exacerbation of the conflict. By negotiating exclusively with the warlords, the UN effectively granted them greater prestige than their positions warranted. This point is made most vociferously by Prendergast, who argues that the UN should never have negotiated with the warlords for the deployment of peacekeepers, as to do so simply elevated their importance.[28] In January 1993 the UN sponsored a peace conference to which it invited only the 14 warlords who were vying for power, failing to include Somali intellectuals and clan elders. These elders were essential to any attempts to negotiate peace, because only they could settle disputes over issues such as property and grazing rights. Nevertheless, the UN and UNITAF continued the policy of sidelining such groups in negotiations, only realising the error of their ways following horrific incidents like those of 12 July 1993, in which the suspected headquarters of one of the warlords, General Mohammed Farah Aideed, was attacked by UN and US forces. In the ensuing battle more than 50 Somalis died and another 170 were left injured, including key religious leaders and clan elders.[29] These traditional elders, belonging to a number of Somali tribes, were believed to have been meeting to develop a negotiating strategy with UNOSOM II. Bradbury has speculated that 'the killing of these people prevented an early resolution of the conflict'.[30]

The UN's failure to understand the cultural context of its operations also led it to implement inappropriate policies in its relations with the Somali clans. This was never more evident than in its attempts to arrest Aideed, the leader of the clan it believed responsible for attacks on UN peacekeepers on 4 June 1993. The UN even offered a $25,000 reward for his capture. However, such a policy was inappropriate for two reasons. Firstly, as Anderson asserts, this personalisation of the conflict was never understood by the Somali people because the traditional clan structure of Somali society dictates that an attack on one member is an attack on all. If one member of a clan is guilty of a crime, the whole clan assumes responsibility. Therefore, when the UN attacked Aideed, it automatically attacked all the members of his Habir-Gedir sub-clan.[31] Secondly, by offering a reward for Aideed's capture the UN effectively insulted ordinary Somalis, who were simply reminded of their previous experiences under colonialism.

So, as the above accounts make apparent, the UN's negotiations with the local factions in Somalia were proceeding in a cultural context which the organisation did not fully understand. This cultural context, as in the previous cases covered by this chapter, determined not only the local factions' negotiating strategies but also their reactions to UN policies. When the UN finally realised its mistakes, accepting in 1994 that national reconciliation would be better fostered through the 'framework of the traditional structures' of Somali society, it was simply too late in the day to save the UN operations.

CONCLUSION

As this chapter has illustrated, when the UN negotiates with internal parties involved in civil wars, it needs to take account of the cultural context within which those negotiations are taking place. In so doing it is not the intention of the author to criticise those who have attempted to negotiate peace agreements in the extremely complex and precarious circumstances that characterise civil wars. Rather, the intention of this chapter is simply to draw attention to the importance of cultural sensitivity by an organisation which by its very nature is prone to understand and conduct negotiations in a manner typical of the Western-orientated 'diplomatic culture'.

The importance of culture in the process of understanding is elucidated by Cohen when he states:

> From characterising culture as a shared body of meaning, it is but a short step to realising that a boundary that contains may also be a barrier that excludes ... culture constructs reality; different cultures construct reality differently; communication across cultures pits different constructions of reality against each other.[32]

This is as true for an international organisation negotiating with internal parties from a separate culture as it is for two states negotiating in the international arena. To ignore the significance of this is to fail to appreciate how the negotiating positions and subsequent actions of internal parties are determined by their culturally constructed realities. In all four operations covered by this chapter the UN exhibited tendencies

13

to do just that – tendencies which allowed the organisation to continue to employ inappropriate negotiating strategies.

However, as the account of the UN's involvement in Mozambique illustrates, cultural sensitivity can make a significant, if not vital, difference to the outcome of its peacekeeping missions. By learning to negotiate within the culture of the internal parties, the UN was able to avoid a repeat of the Angolan tragedy. Similar exhibits of cultural sensitivity may do the same in the future. Nevertheless, international organisations like the UN must be careful not to expect local traditional negotiating methods always to be more successful. This was made apparent in Somalia when even after the UN attempted to foster reconciliation conferences through the traditional structures of Somali society, clan leaders like Aideed still showed a tendency to circumvent negotiations in order to maintain their positions.[33] So, the UN cannot always expect local traditional techniques to be any more successful in the short term. Yet, if the organisation fails to take account of the cultural context in which it negotiates, then the scales of probability swing heavily in the direction of failure.

NOTES

1. R. Licklider, quoted in T.D. Mason and P.J. Fett, 'How Civil Wars End', *Journal of Conflict Resolution*, 40: 4 (1996), p. 547.
2. S. Bailey, quoted in R. Cooper and M. Berdal, 'Outside Intervention in Ethnic Conflicts', *Survival*, 35: 1 (spring 1993), p. 139.
3. The fact that the respective resistance factions were not involved in negotiations did cause problems for the implementation of the respective agreements. Soviet and Cuban forces withdrawing from Afghanistan and Angola both came under fire from resistance members, resulting in a temporary suspension of both operations. In Nicaragua, having not been party to the regional negotiations, the Contras staged attacks designed to interrupt voter registration causing the Sandinista government eventually to break its ceasefire agreement.
4. For an account of 'diplomatic culture' see K. Krause (ed.), *Culture and Security: Multilateralism, Arms Control and Security-building* (London: Frank Cass, 1999), pp. 6–8.
5. These particular operations have been chosen to satisfy a number of criteria: they vary in size and complexity; they are geographically dispersed and culturally varied; and, perhaps most importantly, they are differentiated by their relative records of success and failure.
6. For an account of the UN's increasing involvement in the implementation of the accords see M.J. Anstee, *Orphan of the Cold War* (Basingstoke: Macmillan, 1996).
7. J.E. Pondi, quoted in K. Hart and J. Lewis (eds), *Why Angola Matters* (Cambridge: Cambridge University Press, 1995), p. 41.
8. Anstee, *Orphan of the Cold War*, p. 534.

9. G. Wright, *The Destruction of a Nation – US Policy toward Angola since 1945* (London: Pluto Press, 1997), p. 157. This was corroborated by UNITA's own electoral office which acknowledged that it had made mistakes, including the resumption of violence and an undemocratic stance towards the elections, based on the certain belief that it would win. It also believed that it would have fared disastrously in the second round of elections because it had failed to play an effective role in the election process. See F.O. Hampson, *Nurturing Peace: Why Peace Settlements Succeed or Fail* (Washington, DC: US Institute of Peace Press, 1996), p. 115.

10. V. Brittain, quoted in Hart and Lewis (eds), *Why Angola Matters*, pp. 69, 77.

11. UN document S/25913, 10 June 1993.

12. *The UN and Cambodia 1991–1995* (New York: Department of Public Information, 1995), p. 46.

13. As Roberts notes, however, not all parties found the new arrangements completely to their liking. The United States apparently continued to try to prevent Sihanouk from assuming the position of head of state as late as 15 June. This was after all the internal parties had elected him to the position in the Cambodia assembly. D. Roberts, 'More Honoured in the Breech: Consent and Impartiality in the Cambodian Peacekeeping Operation', in *International Peacekeeping*, 4: 1 (1997), pp. 15–16 and *The UN and Cambodia, 1991–1995*, p. 47.

14. P. Lizee, 'Peacekeeping, Peace-building and the Challenge of Conflict-Resolution in Cambodia', in D. Charters (ed.), *Peacekeeping and the Challenge of Conflict Resolution* (New Brunswick: University of New Brunswick Press, 1994), pp. 135–48.

15. T. Findlay, *Cambodia: The Legacy and Lessons of UNTAC*, SIPRI Research Report No. 9 (Oxford: Oxford University Press, 1995), p. 110.

16. Lizee, 'Peacekeeping', p. 143.

17. D. Roberts, 'More Honoured in the Breech', pp. 8–9.

18. The UN's more involved role in Mozambique was due to a great extent to the insistence of the special representative in Angola who, thinking it probable that she might be transferred to Mozambique, insisted on a more appropriate mandate. See Anstee, *Orphan of the Cold War*.

19. This point is reiterated by Young, who suggests that too much 'has been made … of the absence of a RENAMO political programme because in Western conceptions politics is about programmes, ideological beliefs, calculations of political support from different kinds of groups and so on'. D. Hoile, *Mozambique: Resistance and Freedom* (Mozambique: The Mozambique Institute, 1994), p. 50.

20. Most writers on Mozambique (such as Minter, Vines and Anderson) argue that RENAMO had little if no independent political platform before the peace process started. See W. Minter, *Apartheid's Contras* (Tvl: Witwatersand University Press, 1994), p. 156; and Hoile, *Mozambique*, p. x. See also M. Hall, 'The Mozambican National Resistance (RENAMO): A Study in the Destruction of an African Country', *Africa*, 60: 1 (1990); and H. Anderson, *Mozambique: A War against the People* (Basingstoke: Macmillan, 1992).

21. 'Document 54', *The United Nations and Mozambique 1992–95* (New York: Department of Public Information, 1995), p. 215.

22. C. Crawford, 'Mozambique's Fragile Peace Process Risks too Easy

Derailment', *Financial Times*, 25 January 1994.
23. Brittain, 'A State Made to the UN's Design', in Hart and Lewis (eds), *Why Angola Matters*.
24. Ibid.
25. *Daily Telegraph*, 18 November 1994.
26. UN document, S/25168, 26 January 1994.
27. For a full account of Sahnoun's negotiating strategies see his personal account of the initial months of the Somali operation in M. Sahnoun, *Somalia: The Missed Opportunities* (Washington, DC: US Institute of Peace Press, 1994), p. 5.
28. J. Prendergast, *The Gun Talks Louder than the Vote* (Washington, DC: Centre for Concern, July 1994), p. 22.
29. M. Berdal, 'Fateful Encounter: The United States and UN Peacekeeping', *Survival*, 36: 1 (1994), p. 42.
30. Bradbury, quoted in Prendergast, *The Gun Talks Louder than the Vote*, p. 22.
31. G. Anderson, 'UNOSOM II: Not Failure, Not Success', in D. Daniel and B. Hayes (eds), *Beyond Traditional Peacekeeping* (Basingstoke: Macmillan, 1995), p. 270.
32. R. Cohen, 'Cultural Aspects of International Mediation', in J. Bercovich (ed.), *Resolving International Conflicts* (Boulder, CO: Lynne Rienner, 1996), pp. 109, 111.
33. Attempts by the Imam of Harib to organise a national reconciliation conference in 1994 were to be unsuccessful because Aideed decided after a preliminary agreement that the conference was no longer necessary. This was to the complete surprise of the Imam. UN documents, S/1994/977, 19 August 1994 and S/1994/1166, 14 October 1994.

2

Negotiation in Three Dimensions: Managing the Public Face of International Negotiation

ROBIN BROWN

INTRODUCTION

The contemporary era is commonly described as the information age. All aspects of human society are subject to pressures for change from the tidal wave of innovation in information and communications technologies. Processes of international negotiation and persuasion are no exception. In the view of some analysts we are entering a era of massive change that will revolutionise international affairs (Deibert, 1997; Rosenau, 1990; 1997; Rosecrance, 1996), while others take a more nuanced view (Strobel, 1997; Neumann, 1996; Seib, 1997; Taylor, 1997). Indeed, a fundamental problem in addressing these issues is deciding what we mean by change. More than a century ago the fundamental transformatory impact of the telegraph was being proclaimed, but many aspects of international relationship seem to have evolved rather than being fundamentally transformed (Headrick, 1991).

This chapter explores the way in which contemporary international negotiations are being transformed by new technologies. The central argument is that negotiation is a way of dealing with conflict by controlling who is involved and the sequence in which issues are handled. The emergence of new media are making this control of scope more difficult to achieve, with the result that those involved in negotiation have to think about not just how they will handle the other side but also the ever-expanding audience. These developments are not entirely new. The connection between negotiations and the broader world have always been there, but the management of this dimension becomes a more pressing issue in an environment that is increasingly transparent to the news media and other political actors as a consequence of the diffusion of new information and communication technologies. I shall argue that in an era where communications are ever cheaper and easier, negotiators have to come to terms with the third dimension: the way in which negotiations connect with the world beyond the table. New developments in information and communications allow groups external to the negotiation an ever greater opportunity to exert influence on it. Thus, in formulating a strategy negotiators have to take the public dimension and consequences of their activities into account.

THE THREE DIMENSIONS OF NEGOTIATION

Any negotiation has three dimensions. The first and most obvious is that between the parties undertaking it – across the negotiating table. Secondly, there is the interface that exists between the negotiators and the their employers or constituencies. Thirdly, there is the interface with the wider world – third parties and the public. For historical and conceptual reasons it is the first dimension that has always attracted the most attention in the study of negotiation.

The emphasis on the first dimension is hardly surprising since the outcome of negotiation should be an agreement that satisfies all parties. However, the ability to reach such an agreement depends on the ability to manage the second and third dimensions of negotiation. Can the negotiators produce a deal that keeps their own constituencies happy without an unmanageable degree of pressure from third parties?

The classical image of diplomatic negotiation is a situation where negotiators will sit down in private and thrash out a deal that will be accepted by their respective constituents. Operating in private (or even in secret) will exclude extraneous factors and allow the issues at stake to be handled in an orderly fashion, with trade-offs being made over contentious issues. At the end of the negotiation an agreed text is signed and then ratified. This is an image appropriate to a stable and hierarchical world. Negotiators have authority to negotiate; they are in a position to ensure delivery on promises because their employers in turn enjoy unchallenged authority. Interests and values are clearly specified and do not change over time. This image of negotiation betrays a nostalgia for a world where kings could make agreements that (for instance) allowed them to trade provinces without reference to anyone else. A central element in the development of diplomacy in the twentieth century has been the erosion of this isolation. The autonomy once enjoyed by kings, foreign offices and generals has been eroded by the rise of democracy. In the wake of the First World War some maintained that it was secret diplomacy that gave rise to the conflict; thus, it was argued, diplomacy had to become more open and more accountable (Anderson, 1993).

Although discussions of the problems created by the growing democratisation of negotiation are often found in historical and practical discussions of diplomacy most general discussions of *negotiation* reinforce the focus on the first dimension (e.g. Eban, 1998, Chapter 5). Most of the more reflective discussions of negotiation draw on rational choice or psychological approaches to interaction. There are good reasons for this. One piece of advice commonly found in treatments of negotiation is the need for negotiators to think creatively and flexibly about negotiation. Rational choice theory (Raiffa, 1982) reduces complex issues to relatively simple frameworks and hence suggests possible solutions. It also provides a set of bargaining tactics. A second theoretical approach is to look at negotiation as an exercise in interpersonal skills. Thus the task of the negotiator is to build up a relationship of trust with the interlocutor that will allow the removal of barriers to agreement. Although these two approaches have very different intellectual roots they point in much the same direction towards negotiation as something that happens across a table between individuals or small groups. Isolating negotiation from the broader context to the greatest possible extent allows the negotiators to explore different outcomes and construct packages of measures in which unpalatable concessions on issues are balanced by gains on other issues. Thinking abstractly may then allow the identification of agreements that move beyond the starting positions.

In consequence relatively little attention is given to the second and third dimensions: how do domestic constituencies and third parties respond to processes of negotiation? In international relations the second dimension has recently attracted a growing interest. In a widely cited article Robert Putnam argued that negotiations could be characterised as 'two-level games' (Putnam, 1988). A two-party international negotiation involved Level 1 (the direct interaction between the negotiators) and Level 2 (the interaction between the negotiators and their domestic constituencies). Thus to be successful a negotiation has to produce outcomes that are not only acceptable to the negotiators but are also acceptable 'at home'. The two-level game has become a commonly used metaphor which has stimulated a considerable literature devoted to extending the analysis (Evans, Jacobson and Putnam, 1993). This literature points to a growing awareness of the context within which negotiations take place, but much remains to be done. The impact of third parties, for instance, remains largely neglected.

UNDERSTANDING THE THIRD DIMENSION

In a classic discussion of international negotiation Fred Iklé observed that 'secrecy has two major effects in diplomacy. Firstly, it keeps domestic groups ignorant of the process of negotiation, thereby preventing them from exerting pressures during successive phases of bargaining. Second, it leaves third parties in the dark and thus reduces their influence' (Iklé, 1964, p. 134).

Implicit in this is that lack of secrecy allows domestic groups to exert pressure and allows third parties to increase their influence. Iklé's insight can be profitably placed in a broader theoretical context.

In analysing the workings of the American political system, E.E. Schattschneider argues that political conflict can be thought of as a fight: 'Every fight consists of two parts: (1) the few individuals who are actively engaged at the centre and (2) the audience that is irresistibly attracted to the scene ... the outcome of every conflict is determined by the extent that the audience becomes involved in it.'

Hence, 'if a fight starts, watch the crowd [since] the outcome of all conflict is determined by the scope of its contagion. The number of people involved in any conflict determines what happens; every increase or reduction in the number of participants, affects the result.' The consequence is that 'the most important strategy of politics is concerned with the scope of the conflict ... So great is the change in the nature of any conflict likely to be as a consequence of the widening involvement of people in it that the original participants are apt to lose control of the conflict altogether' (Schattschneider, 1960, pp. 2–3).

Conflicts which are liable to spread have a dynamic of their own, with the original parties unable to control the outcome (Schattschneider, 1960, pp. 2–3). As more people become aware that a decision is to be taken or a 'fight' is in progress, more people have the opportunity to seek to exert influence or to join the conflict. Such a process will not be neutral: the make-up of the audience will determine who benefits from such a process of expansion.

Iklé's advocacy of secrecy can be seen as a particular form of the control of scope. Limiting the range of parties both simplifies negotiation and excludes particular groups. Defining the scope of a negotiation and managing the reaction of those not at the table is a part of any negotiation. The problem is that the result of the information explosion is a 'Schattschneider effect': in a shrinking world it becomes increasingly difficult to maintain the secrecy that Iklé recommends. Negotiations will increasingly be carried out in the glare of publicity, so that it becomes easier for domestic political groups or third parties to exert pressure on the negotiators, who in turn must work harder to deal with the third dimension.

THE CHANGING INTERNATIONAL ENVIRONMENT

As we have already seen, the third-dimension challenge for negotiators is not new: it emerges from two developments. The growth of democracy has been associated with a demand for greater political control over the activities of diplomats and foreign ministries, both from elected politicians and other politically active groups. The impact of these broad social and political changes has been increased by the successive waves of innovation in communications technologies that started around 1840 (Headrick, 1991; Briggs, 1966; Mattelart, 1994). These developments have reduced the autonomy of negotiators from their principals and from other social and political actors. Put simply, ambassadors and other negotiators have found themselves looking over their shoulders (Neumann, 1996).

In the past decade these developments have entered a new phase. Political developments have continued to expand the range of actors involved in and relevant to negotiation. The wave of failed states (Somalia, Sierra Leone, Yugoslavia, Former Soviet Union and so on) have created a set of complex situations where negotiation frequently involves armed groups and political organisations whose credentials are open to question, as is the extent to which they actually represent anyone (Langford, 1999). To complicate the picture still further, these situations are often accompanied by the large-scale involvement of humanitarian aid organisations from many countries. This illustrates a wider issue: namely, the increasing involvement of non-governmental organisations in many aspects of diplomacy if not formal negotiation (Salamon, 1994). Because these organisations exist to advance specific causes their involvement can complicate the task of managing negotiations.

These groups come into play in an environment where the communications revolution has made its mark. Political groupings increasingly have access to the latest communications technology such as the internet, satellite phones and satellite television. This allows them to do two things. First, to gather information on their environment – a comment by a British politician that finds itself into an on-line version of a newspaper or the BBC website is available globally; similarly, television pictures diffuse globally. The ease of gathering material may create new exploitable opportunities: for instance, knowing that a meeting is taking place creates the possibility of influencing its outcome. At the same time the new

21

communications environment allows groups to reach out to make their own views clear or to mobilise supporters, whether by phone, the internet, e-mail distribution lists, or by giving interviews or mounting actions via the media. Understanding how to make use of the new communications environment is increasingly diffused. A widely cited example is the success of the Mexican Zapatistas in making use of the new technology. The Zapatistas were able to advance their cause, or at least to protect themselves from the reaction of the Mexican state by publicising their activities and creating political pressures on the government that inhibited a repressive response. The lesson is that governments cannot simply count the strength of an opponent by how many men it can muster on the ground (Ronfeldt and Martinez, 1997).

Even in the absence of new political actors, the dynamics of negotiation are becoming more vulnerable to the changing organisation of the media. The relationship between media and foreign affairs has always been difficult in cases of low-intensity conflict, but in recent years a number of developments have intensified the potential for conflict between media and negotiators. One factor in this is the technological developments that have opened the way for expansion in the volume of news output. Less than two decades ago, British television consisted of three terrestrial channels, with limited daytime broadcasting hours. Today British viewers can choose from two UK-oriented 24-hour news services in Sky News and BBC News 24. They can also access global and regional news services, including CNN, CNBC and Bloomberg, not to mention foreign-language news services. Additionally, the internet provides unlimited information sources, ranging from the esoteric to the mainstream.

In a subtle way, 24-hour news changes the dynamics of reporting. Faced with hours of programming to fill, stations constantly seek the latest developments in an ongoing story, even if that development tends to amount to nothing more than rumour. The problem is reinforced by the intense competition between commercially-funded operations to be first with the news. Competition marks a return to a 'stop the presses' mentality. In the old media environment broadcast media ran two or three bulletins a day, making the production of news relatively leisurely by today's standards and giving the opportunity to review the content of bulletins. In a 24-hour competitive environment the commercial advantages of going first opens the way for reporting that might have seemed irresponsible in the past (MacGregor, 1997; Alleyne, 1997).

This competitive pressure is reinforced by the emergence of the technology of news-gathering. Lightweight cameras and satellite dishes allow news-gatherers to report from inaccessible parts of the world and to get their stories back almost immediately. Journalists can then pop up almost anywhere. During the Falklands War the ability of journalists to send reports home was limited by their dependence on military communications and logistic systems, whereas contemporary communications systems are cheap enough to put satellite communications systems into the hands of even the smallest news operation. Current and future developments will only increase the transparency of the world. The improving quality and falling prices of digital video equipment, together with the developing capacity of global networks, means that the ability to shoot and gather footage from almost anywhere will increase. And the diffusion of video cameras means that footage can appear from the most unexpected parts of the world. Another technology that deserves mention is the emergence of commercial satellite surveillance. As resolution increases and costs fall, overhead imagery will become a routine part of the news-gathering arsenal (Livingston, 1999).

The combination of news-gathering technology with the means to diffuse it inevitably means that negotiation will, at least potentially, take place under the glare of publicity. The logic of Schattschneider's analysis gains in power over Iklé's prescription. More people in more places become aware of negotiations and gain the potential to influence them.

The type of influence that such people can exert will be influenced by three aspects of media working practices. First, media reporting is dominated not by what is true but by the *story*. In order to make sense of a complex world in a limited time, journalists (often unconsciously) try to fit a complex reality into a small number of standard frames. The use of the term 'story' gives a clue to the logic of reporting practice. Following the tenets of drama a good story has a plot, characters, a beginning, middle and end, and conflict. Of course the real world very often has none of these. What happens is that a given situation gets shoehorned into a grossly simplified and overdramatised format. Media reporting seeks to identify good guys and bad guys and to eliminate ambiguity. It prefers clearcut outcomes, 'disasters' or 'triumphs', to more complex realities (Darnton, 1975; Tarrow, 1994, Chapter 7). Second, reporting happens in time. Because news is supposed to be new this reinforces the drive to simplify but also creates a pressure to find new developments even if they are absent (Patterson, 1998). The pressure of time leads on to a third issue: the use of sources. How do journalists find out what is going on? They ask people. Whom do they ask? The most important sources tend to be, inevitably, official spokespersons predominantly of their own nationality. For example, journalists reporting for a network like Sky News will tend to turn initially to UK official sources for information (Ericson, 1989; Sigal, 1973). While this logic is important, the developments cited above tend to undermine the ability of official spokespersons to control the framing of unfolding stories. The ability of news-gatherers to gain access to remote areas and to talk to representatives of other involved parties creates a challenge that is difficult to manage. The fact that many contemporary international events are ambiguous makes it more difficult for governmental actors to exercise control over news operations.

Thus any negotiation takes place in an environment that is potentially transparent, where the reactions of those not at the negotiating table may be more difficult to manage than in the past. These developments reinforce what students of negotiation tend to regard as the pathologies, as those involved in negotiation attach greater importance to events outside than across the table. The implications of these developments can be seen in three recent cases.

The first case illustrates the benefits of secrecy. The announcement of the negotiations between Israel and the Palestine Liberation Organisation (PLO) that resulted in the Oslo Accords of 20 August 1993 took the world by surprise. Here was a perfect example of the benefits of secret diplomacy in their most extreme form. This was not just a case of the content of negotiation being kept secret but of the very existence of negotiation itself. Thus, the announcement took not only the news media and the public at large by surprise, but also the US government. By operating in secret the parties were able to craft a deal that could be presented to the rest of the world as a *fait accompli*, where the fact of the agreement was the most powerful reply to critics and opponents. By operating in secret, objections to the fact of the negotiations as well as their content could be negated. At the point where the existence of the deal was revealed, the Israeli government's public stance was that it would not talk to the terrorists of the PLO, and the open negotiations were stalled. By breaking away from the public positions the back-channel Oslo diplomacy created a space for change that opened the way to the creation of an autonomous Palestinian political entity (Eban, 1998, Chapter 5). The progress of the peace process during the period since speaks volumes about the complexity of managing contentious negotiations in the full glare of publicity.

The second example is the failure of the negotiations over the Multilateral Agreement on Investment (MAI). This was a project by which the 29 members of the Organisation for Economic Cooperation and Development (OECD) would develop a common set of rules to regulate international investment. Although not strictly secret, the negotiations attracted little attention until January 1997, when a confidential draft of the treaty was posted on the internet (OECD, 1997). This was a starting point for a concerted campaign against the treaty in many of the OECD member countries. What the internet did was to ease the task of mobilising against the treaty and the OECD governments found themselves subject to growing public criticism from a variety of sources. Criticism came from environmentalists and labour groups, as well as local governments and legislators who felt that they had been excluded from a process that had important implications and, in the view of some activists, threatened democracy and sovereignty. Under pressure the negotiations faltered. The governments had hoped to have an agreed text by the OECD ministerial meeting in April 1998, but as the negotiations became more salient existing disagreements became more obvious, resulting in the announcement of a six-month review period to allow consultation with non-governmental actors. By the time negotiations resumed in October, France had announced its withdrawal from them, and by the end of the year the whole project had been abandoned (OECD, 1998a; 1998b; 1998c). What the internet did was to accelerate the whole process, but timing is important in negotiation. Had objections been raised to an agreed text they might have lost their force. Hence, this appears to be a clear example of the increasing ability of excluded actors to involve themselves in the process.

The third example comes from events surrounding the Kosovo conflict. During the negotiations at Rambouillet, prior to the beginning of the NATO bombing campaign, the European and American mediators sought to isolate the negotiation from its broader context by seeking to discourage contact between the negotiators and the outside world. The daily press conferences were uninformative; at various points advisers to the Kosovan delegation were excluded; no facilities were provided for journalists; and the Yugoslavian delegation complained about the lack of secure communications facilities. The mediators' objective was to isolate the talks in order to force the delegations to focus on the matter in hand and to reduce the political pressures on them. Ironically, it was the delegations that chafed under these restrictions, to the extent that diplomatic sources were complaining about the delegates' use of mobile phones! Ensuring a favourable spin on developments for their domestic audiences seemed to be more important than focusing on the process itself. As the American mediator Christopher Hill commented, 'this is an era of cell phones and that has changed the world of sequestered conferences' (French Ministry of Foreign Affairs, 1999). James Rubin, the State Department spokesman, put it more bluntly: the delegates should 'keep their nose to the grindstone and their hands off their cell phones and do the work that's necessary to reach an agreement' (State Department, 1999; Walker, 1999; Trueheart, 1999).

In each of these three cases the relationship with the world beyond the negotiating table was crucial to the outcome. In the Oslo case, isolation allowed the creation of a *fait accompli* that marginalised opposition groups with a completed deal. The MAI negotiations failed to produce such a deal because growing exposure mobilised opposition both to the purpose of the agreement in general and to specific elements. It might be argued that the MAI negotiations would have been more successful either with a greater degree of secrecy to produce a deal that could then be sold by governments, or by a greater degree of openness through which governments could draw interested parties into the process. Either approach would have required a more coherent strategy for dealing with the presentation of the negotiations. Finally, the Rambouillet negotiations produced what the Western powers must have regarded as a successful result – the acceptance of the accord by the Kosovan side – but the whole process proved to be more protracted and difficult than was expected. This was mainly due to the inability of the mediators to isolate the negotiations and impose a settlement.

LESSONS FOR NEGOTIATION

What lessons about negotiation should we learn from this analysis? Firstly both Iklé and Schattschneider are right. Secrecy does simplify the negotiators' task, but the impact of the information age is to make effective secrecy more difficult to achieve. Hence, negotiators have to be aware of the public face of the negotiation at all its stages. Although the success of the Oslo negotiations stemmed in part from the fact that very few people were aware that the negotiations were going on, such a level of secrecy is rarely feasible. Furthermore, the fact that negotiations require such levels of isolation will tend to call into question the legitimacy of outcomes – an MAI produced in total secrecy would have been hard to sell.

A situation where the fact of negotiation is known will be more typical. Hence designing a media- or public-information strategy must be an integral part of the design of the negotiation. Of course many practical applications of the art of negotiation are of little interest to anyone but the parties directly concerned, but the more important the subject matter and the more high-profile the negotiators, the more negotiations will become subject to the attentions of outsiders. The nature of the information strategy will depend on the relationship between the parties. The task will be greatly simplified if a common approach can be agreed – for instance joint press briefings or an agreement to say nothing. However, the feasibility of saying nothing needs to be balanced with the nature of the media. If the media is excluded from almost all negotiating, journalists then develop an insatiable appetite for information. Deploying a journalist and film crew to cover a negotiation involves a considerable cost, and news organisations will demand reports regardless of developments. Faced with a situation where no reliable information is available the media will be more prone to speculate or report rumours that may soon take on a factual appearance for the constituency of one side or the other. Speculation that the negotiation is deadlocked or that a breakthrough is imminent will emerge – which will be undesirable in the context of a protracted encounter.

A situation where negotiators cannot reach agreement about the way to handle the public face of the negotiation, or where that agreement is violated, is more difficult. The essential point is that if one side is talking to the media and the other is not, the former will be in a position to define the content and progress of the negotiation in a way that suits them, and by doing so to create pressures that will rebound on the negotiation. For instance the opponent's position can be made to look unreasonable in the eyes of third parties, or even in the sight of their constituency. Thus, public-information strategies, at a minimum, must take account of the negative impact of an opponent's strategy. At the same time, communication becomes a strategic activity by which the perceptions of the other side and also the home side can be influenced. For many senior decision-makers media reports perform a dual role. First, they provide a check on what is being reported through channels. Second, the media are the key source of information for the general public and for the political community. Hence what the media are saying about a negotiation has to be carefully monitored since that will be the reality for most people, even if those reports bear little relation to what is actually going on around the negotiating table.

Thus, the negotiating team will need to think carefully about what it needs to be saying, to whom, and at what point in time. In an international context how to handle journalists from both sides and from neutrals will have to be considered. Although it is important to brief the 'home team', it should be remembered that in the contemporary world attempting to say different things to different audiences may rapidly lead to confusion as media reports are picked up and compared. The other side in a conflictual negotiation will be carefully scrutinising public utterances for clues as to strategies and positions (Cohen, 1981).

The implication of the greater transparency of the negotiation environment is that negotiators will have to think about their job in a broader way, to become more aware of the public face and not simply of their interlocutors. What they say and don't say to the media will be closely scrutinised. Although they may resent it, diplomats and soldiers charged with negotiations have to learn, in the way that politicians have learned, to navigate the media jungle. Over the past four decades democratic politicians have developed a set of strategies that reflect the reality that modern politics is media politics (Kernell, 1986; Rose, 1988; Cockerell, 1988; Jones, 1995; Kurtz, 1998). It is only in the last decade that the emergence of all-news television has begun to give the media a role in international politics that is relatively independent of government, and diplomacy has not yet adapted to this environment. This learning process was symbolised by the arrival of Alastair Campbell (Tony Blair's press secretary) at NATO during the Kosovo conflict, with the mission to improve the presentation of the Alliance campaign (Oborne, 1999, pp. 204–6). The expertise developed in the cut-and-thrust of domestic politics was now to be applied to the world of diplomacy.

Negotiation has always been part of the broader political environment, and current developments simply reinforce this point, but at the same time it has often proved difficult to integrate negotiation into a broader political strategy. Cold War commentators used to lament the difficulty that democracies had with talking and fighting at the same time (Brodie, 1973). It might be suggested that the issue is now how to talk, fight and spin at the same time.

CONCLUSIONS

Negotiations have always been part of a broader world – an obvious point but one that is often forgotten. The logic of media developments is to make that linkage tighter and more immediate, and negotiators have to recognise that this external face of the process deserves as much care as the internal face. A well-handled public face may feed back into the negotiation in a constructive way, but mistakes through lack of attention may have precisely the opposite effect. Negotiations are often an attempt to break the logic of events by stepping away from them, but this is more difficult to accomplish than in the past. From the negotiator's standpoint this may make his or her job more difficult, but if negotiations are to produce viable and lasting solutions then there is no alternative.

REFERENCES

Alleyne, Mark (1997), *News Revolution: Political and Economic Decisions about Global Information* (New York: St Martin's Press).

Anderson, M.S. (1993), *The Rise of Modern Diplomacy 1450–1919* (Harlow: Longman).

Briggs, Asa (1966), *The Communications Revolution* (Leeds: University of Leeds Press).

Brodie, Bernard (1973), *War and Politics* (New York: Macmillan).

Caporaso, James A. (1997), 'Across the Great Divide: Integrating Comparative and International Politics', *International Studies Quarterly*, 41: 4 (December).

Cockerell, Michael (1988), *Live from Number 10: The Inside Story of Prime Ministers and Television* (London: Faber & Faber).

Cohen, Raymond (1981), *International Politics: The Rules of the Game* (Harlow: Longman).

Deibert, Ronald (1997), *Parchment, Printing and Hypermedia: Communication in World Order Transformation* (New York: Columbia University Press).

Eban, Abba (1998), *Diplomacy for the Next Century* (New Haven, CT: Yale University Press).

Ericson, R.V. (1989), *Negotiating Control: A Study of News Sources* (Toronto: University of Toronto).

Evans, Peter B., Jacobson, Harold K. and Putnam, Robert D. (eds) (1993), *Double-edged Diplomacy: International Bargaining and Domestic Politics* (Berkeley, CA: University of California Press).

French Ministry of Foreign Affairs (1999), press briefing with Rambouillet negotiators, 9 February.

Headrick, Daniel R. (1991), *The Invisible Weapon: Telecommunications and International Politics, 1851–1945* (New York: Oxford University Press).

Iklé, Fred C. (1964), *How Nations Negotiate* (New York: Harper & Row).

Jones, N. (1995), *Soundbites and Spin Doctors: How Politicians Manipulate the Media – and Vice Versa* (London: Cassell).

Kernell, Samuel (1986), *Going Public: New Strategies of Presidential Leadership* (Washington DC: Congressional Quarterly Press).

Kurtz, Howard (1998), *Spin Cycle: Inside the Clinton Propaganda Machine* (London: Pan).

Langford, Tonya (1999), 'Things Fall Apart: State Failure and the Politics of Intervention', *International Studies Review*, 1: 1 (spring).

Livingston, Steven (1999), 'The New Information Environment and Diplomacy', paper presented at the International Studies Association Annual Convention, Washington DC (February).

MacGregor, Brent (1997), *Live, Direct and Biased? Making Television News in the Satellite Age* (London: Edward Arnold).

Mattelart, Armand (1994), *Mapping World Communication: War, Progress, Culture*, trans. Susan Emanuel and James A. Cohen (Minnesota: University of Minnesota Press).

Neuman, Johanna (1996), *Lights, Camera, War: Is Media Technology Driving International Politics?* (New York: St Martins Press).

Oborne, Peter (1999), *Alastair Campbell: New Labour and the Rise of the Media Class* (London: Aurum).

OECD (1997), Draft of the Multilateral Agreement on Investment, 13 January, posted at *www.essential.org/monitor/MAI/contents.html* (accessed 15 September 1999).

—— (1998a), Ministerial Statement on the MAI, *www.oecd.org/news_and_events/nw98-50a.htm*, 28 April (accessed 15 September 1999).

—— (1998b), Opening Statement by Mr Donald J. Johnston, Secretary-General, Consultation on MAI, *www.oecd.org/news_and_events/nw98-100a.htm*, 22 October (accessed 15 September 1999).

—— (1998c), 'Negotiations on the MAI are No Longer Taking Place', press release at *www.oecd.org/news_and_events/nw98-114a.htm*, 3 December (accessed 15 September 1999).

Patterson, Thomas E. (1998), 'Time and News: The Media's Limitations as an Instrument of Democracy', *International Political Science Review*, 19: 1 (January).

Raiffa, Howard (1982), *The Art and Science of Negotiation* (Cambridge, MA: Harvard University Press).

Putnam, Robert D. (1988), 'Diplomacy and Domestic Politics: The Logic of Two-Level Games', *International Organisation*, 42: 3 (summer).

Ronfeldt, David and Martinez, Armando (1997), 'A Comment on the Zapatista Netwar', in John Arquilla and David Ronfeldt (eds), *In Athena's Camp: Preparing for Conflict in the Information Age* (Santa Monica, CA: RAND Corporation).

Rose, Richard (1988), *The Postmodern Presidency* (Chatham, NJ: Chatham House).

Rosecrance, Richard N. (1996), 'The Virtual State', *Foreign Affairs*, 75: 4 (July/August).

Rosenau, James N. (1990), *Turbulence in World Politics: A Theory of Change and Continuity* (Hemel Hempstead: Harvester/Wheatsheaf).

—— (1997), *Along the Domestic–Foreign Frontier: Exploring Governance in a Turbulent World* (Cambridge: Cambridge University Press).

State Department (1999), daily press briefing, 9 February.

Salamon, Lester M. (1994), 'The Global Associational Revolution: The Rise of the Third Sector on the World Scene', *Foreign Affairs*, 73: 4 (July/August).

Schattschneider, E.E. (1960), *The Semisovereign People: A Realist's View of Democracy in America* (Fort Worth, TX: Harcourt Brace, Jovanich).

Seib, Philip (1997), *Headline Diplomacy: How News Coverage Affects Foreign Policy* (New York: Praeger).

Sigal, Leon V. (1973), *Reporters and Officials: The Organisation and Politics of Newsmaking* (Lexington, MA: Heath).

Strobel, Warren P. (1997), *Late-breaking Foreign Policy: The News Media's Influence on Foreign Policy* (Washington, DC: United States Institute of Peace, 1997).

Tarrow, Sidney (1994), *Power in Movement: Social Movements, Collective Action and Politics* (Cambridge: Cambridge University Press).

Taylor, Philip M. (1997), *Global Communications, International Affairs and the Media since 1945* (London: Routledge).

Truehart, Charles (1999), 'Serbs and Kosovars Begin "Serious" Talks', *International Herald Tribune*, 8 February.

Walker, Tom (1999), 'Mobile Threat to Kosovo Diplomacy', *The Times*, 9 February.

Wolfsfeld, Gadi (1997), *The Media and Political Conflict: News From the Middle East* (Cambridge: Cambridge University Press).

3

Breaking the Impasse: Negotiation and Mediation Strategies

BRAD McRAE

In his book *To End a War* which describes the negotiating to end the war in Bosnia-Herzegovina, Richard Holbrooke said: 'A great deal of negotiation is improvisation within the framework of a general goal.' In this chapter we will look at how successful negotiation to resolve intense military disputes rests heavily on improvisation within the framework of a well-developed model of dispute-resolution. The model in question is Lawrence Susskind's three-stage model, as described in his book, *Breaking the Impasse*. We shall look at examples from national and international conflicts to see how the model can be applied. As successful application of the model rests heavily on the practitioner's ability to 'think outside of the box', the chapter concludes with advice to help all of us learn to think more creatively.

The three stages in Susskind's model are:

Stage 1: Pre-negotiation;

Stage 2: Negotiation;

Stage 3: Implementation/post-negotiation.

A thorough examination of each component of the model is beyond the scope of this chapter, so only selected components will be used here to demonstrate its effectiveness. (For a full analysis of each stage, readers should consult Susskind and Cruickshank, 1988.)

STAGE 1: PRE-NEGOTIATION

Stage 1: Pre-negotiation

- How to convene the meeting and other ways to get started
- Ground rules and guidelines for group process including confidentiality
- Defining the role of and making a contract with the mediator/facilitator
- Representation and inclusiveness
- Scheduling
- How to work with the press
- How to use joint fact-finding
- Developing a framing statement

Meeting of the three presidents: the importance of knowing how to convene a meeting

We will now turn our attention to one of the first tasks in Stage 1 – convening the participants. This is aptly illustrated by Carl Bildt's (1998) description of how he endeavoured to convene a meeting of the three co-presidents of Bosnia-Herzegovina. As High Representative, Bildt's task was to oversee the civilian implementation of the civilian tasks of the Dayton Peace Accord. Among the skills that he used were the following: preparation; attention to detail; shuttle diplomacy; knowing the parties; flexibility and inventiveness; risk-taking; foresight, and how to use a BATNA (best alternative to a negotiated agreement). Bildt describes his attempts to convene a meeting of the three presidents in his book *Peace Journey* (1998):

> By lunchtime the next day – back in Sarajevo – there was a sense of mounting crisis ... [There] had been no fewer than five meetings, and there was still total deadlock on the issue of the venue of the first meeting. They were, literally, miles apart. The Serbs had just said that they could accept a building on the IEBL (Inter Entity Boundary Line) that had three different entrances and exits for each of the three members of the Presidency. Knowing the state of the ruins along the IEBL and the former confrontation line, it would have been difficult to find a building with as few as three holes in the walls ...

We tried the US idea of the Konak house ... [But] the Serbs said that it was an insult, since this was a building that they associated with five hundred years of Turkish oppression. Most other people, however, remember it as the building to which the body of Archduke Franz Josef was brought after he was shot by a Serb nationalist in 1914. Whatever the history, it was another dead end (p. 280).

Then, on the Sunday, September 29 came the official certification by the OSCE [Organisation for Security and Cooperation in Europe] mission of the election results. I knew now was the time to act fast. If we lost momentum now, it could be lost for a very long time to come, possibly even forever. I wanted to get some sort of momentum going ... to show everyone that we were moving forward. But how? (pp. 280–1)

... we went through all of the options and possibilities and venues once again ... [There was] a small new hotel that had just reopened, located where the city came to an end and the road to Pale entered its first tunnel. It was called Hotel Saraj ... [Krajisnik, representing the Bosnian Serbs] could maintain that it was hardly Sarajevo. Izetbegovic [representing Bosnia-Herzegovina] could claim that it was a central location, only a stone's throw from the oldest parts of the city ... and Zubak, representing the Bosnian Croats was also agreeable to meeting at the hotel.

I couriered a letter suggesting the site to the three Presidents and that we would convene the meeting at 3 p.m. In a matter of minutes Izebegovic flatly rejected the suggested location. He would not come.

I held firm and thought that we still had a 50/50 chance of success. (p. 282)

It was important to have Zubak in place at the hotel just before 3 p.m. This would send an initial signal to the others. He duly arrived, climbed the stairs and entered a specially prepared room where he waited. Shortly afterwards, I got confirmation from Pale that the Bosnian Serbs' cars were on their way down the road towards Sarajevo. [We were working on Izetbegovic over the telephone.] We told him that a meeting with Zubak and Krajisnik but with him refusing would look very bad. All the Contact Group governments would denounce him in strong terms. (p. 282)

[The Serbs arrived twenty minutes later.] I went in to Krajisnik and chatted about the weather, but without much success. He wanted to know why Izetbegovic was not there. I mumbled something, indicating that he was on his way. Krajisnik knew that Izetbegovic's journey would not take more than five minutes. When ten minutes had passed, the atmosphere became increasingly tense. Krajisnik said that he had been cheated, that we had not been honest with him and that we were merely trying to humiliate him. In the middle of all this, Izebegovic stated that as a condition for his attendance, Krajisnik would have to accept certain new phrases, in advance, of the proposed joint statement. I knew that this would not work out, but that was a later question. I agreed to write down the text and present it as a proposal and that was all. Krajisnik was getting angry. He said that he did not intend to wait any longer, and ordered his security people to prepare for his departure. He was angry – and he had every right to be. (pp. 282–3)

The Americans had exerted all of the pressure at their disposal. Izetbegovic was on his way. At least, that was what I desperately hoped. The seconds and minutes passed extremely slowly. We were hanging in the air between significant success and disastrous failure. But Izetbegovic finally arrived, ascended the stairs and entered his room. (p. 283)

[We had managed to get all three co-presidents] ... into the same building at the same time and in Sarajevo. Their staff reassured them that they were all in the same corridor. Now we had to get them into the same room at one end of the corridor, and preferably keep them there for a while. We checked out the Spartan conference room with the staff of all three co-presidents. There was a round table and three chairs and some mineral water. We had taken down all paintings and pictures from the walls. I did not want to risk a series of history lessons and hang-ups because of some landscape. (p. 283)

Now we just had to get them out of their three rooms and into the conference room. Izetbegovic did not want to go in first – he would enter the room only after the others. This was clearly unacceptable to his potential colleagues, who therefore stubbornly stayed in their room. We suddenly had a new issue to tackle. We ran back and forth along the corridor, trying to find a solution. The only way was to get everyone out in the corridor at the same time and then move them as simultaneously as possible into the conference room. Everyone accepted this, on condition that we could ensure that it would be simultaneous and that there would be no cheating. Certainly, we said, and arranged for the security guards to knock on the three doors at the same time. And – wonder of wonders! – they walked out into the same corridor, in the same building, in the same city, and all at the same time. (p. 283)

34

STAGE 2: NEGOTIATION

The same type of creativity and ingenuity that Carl Bildt applied in Stage 1, in convening the three co-presidents, must also be applied in Stage 2.

Stage 2: Negotiation

- Agenda-setting
- Identifying/exploring interests
- Inventing options
- Packaging: exploring possible trades, suggesting possible packages for the parties to consider
- Collaborative model-building
- Written agreements
- Binding the parties
- Ratification

The Sarajevo airport negotiation

The Sarajevo airport negotiation provides a useful illustration of Stage 2 of Susskind's model. It took place at a time when Bosnia-Herzegovina was in the midst of a devastating civil war. The Bosnian Serbian forces had full occupation of Sarajevo airport. Major-General Lewis MacKenzie was the operational commander for UNPROFOR (United Nations Protection Force) in Sarajevo. He received notification that President Mitterrand was going to make a state visit and would be landing at Sarajevo airport in approximately two hours and 20 minutes. This would have been an insurmountable problem for MacKenzie and the UN forces for the following reasons. First, the Bosnian Serbs occupied the airport and the airport was being used as a base to shell the Bosnian Muslims. The Bosnian Muslims, in turn, were shelling the Bosnian Serbs at the airport. Second, sides of the airport were mined, there were large craters in the runway, as a result of the constant shelling, and the runway was littered with shrapnel and other debris. Third, there were no landing aids because they had all been destroyed. Lastly, there was a good chance that each side might attempt to kill the president during the shelling of the airport and try to blame his death on the other.

MacKenzie decided that two hours and 20 minutes was insufficient time, so he negotiated a 12-hour delay. He then decided that landing by jet was out of the question because there wasn't enough time to clear the runway of hazards. However, there was enough time to clear a small section for a helicopter landing. MacKenzie got all sides to agree to a ceasefire and reminded them that if anything happened to President Mitterrand, he would personally see to it that whoever harmed the president would get full credit for it on CNN. On the other hand, giving up the airport would give the Serbs some badly needed good publicity.

MacKenzie and the UN forces were able to secure the airport for President Mitterrand's visit. Mitterrand met with the presidents of Bosnia-Herzegovina and the president of the Bosnian Serbs in an effort to get them to negotiate a ceasefire. He also met with the French troops stationed in Sarajevo and with the personnel representing the other 29 countries.

MacKenzie then thought that if the UN was able to secure the airport for President Mitterrand's visit to Sarajevo, why not negotiate to keep the airport under UN auspices and use it to bring in humanitarian aid for all sides? (This was to prove to be a much more difficult negotiation.)

However, all three sides – Serbs, Muslims and Croats – were concerned that weapons would be smuggled in along with the humanitarian aid. Since no one trusted anyone else, they finally agreed that a member from each of the three sides would inspect the contents of all planes that landed at the Sarajevo airport. It appeared as though an agreement that was acceptable to all three parties was on the table. A copy of that agreement appears below (MacKenzie, 1993):

Sarajevo Airport Responsibilities

At 1800 hours Monday 29 June 1992 UNPROFOR assumed responsibility for the Sarajevo airport from the 'Serbian Democratic Republic'. The Presidency of Bosnia-Herzegovina and the 'Serbian Democratic Republic' undertake to ensure the security of the airport by guaranteeing that they will not shoot at, shell, attack, or occupy the airport during the presence of UNPROFOR. Any breach whatsoever of this undertaking will be considered a clear indication that the violator does not wish the airport to open and is prepared to accept the international consequences.

Read, understood and agreed:

[signatories] Dr Ganic, the Presidency, Bosnia-Herzegovina; L.W. MacKenzie, Major-General, UNPROFOR; Professor Koljevic, 'Serbian Democratic Republic'.

However, at the last minute, the whole agreement began to unravel:

'Ganic refused to sign any agreement that included the name "Serbian Democratic Republic". MacKenzie explained that quotation marks around the name indicated an unofficial status. He refused to budge and we debated the point for over an hour' (MacKenzie, 1993, p. 268).

The opening of the airport was about to fail because of a disagreement over a matter of principle. Dr Ganic stated that if he signed the document as it stood, it would be tantamount to agreeing that Bosnia-Herzegovina should be partitioned, and it was his government's position that it should not be partitioned. They had reached a critical point in the negotiations to secure the Sarajevo airport for humanitarian aid, and it was all coming apart due to principles that each side said were non-negotiable. Instinctively, MacKenzie knew that they might never again have such a good chance of reaching an agreement. He would have to use all his negotiating abilities and be as creative and flexible as possible if he were to get all the parties to agree. MacKenzie explained his solution as follows: 'I told Ganic that I would produce two documents, one signed by himself and me, the other by a representative from Karadzic's side and me. In the document for his signature, I would change "Serbian Democratic Republic" to "General Mladic's Military Forces". Ganic agreed and signed' (MacKenzie, 1993, p. 268).

In one of the most important negotiations of the civil war, Sarajevo airport was now open to bring in humanitarian aid. Without the use of independent verification, without showing the Bosnian Serbs that opening the airport was in their long-term best interests, and without the flexibility that allowed MacKenzie to use two agreements rather than one, the airport would not have been opened.

The Sarajevo airport negotiation is a prime example of how creative thinking can break the deadlock in a seemingly intractable negotiation. Another example of successful Stage 2 negotiations is found in the Kilometre 101 negotiations.

Kilometre 101: the 1973 October war and the subsequent peace negotiations

The Kilometre 101 negotiations took place after the October 1973 war between Israel and Egypt. These negotiations are important because they demonstrate many of the conditions that are necessary if we are to help resolve protracted, identity-based conflicts. Among the negotiating principles that were employed to bring about progress were (1) the use of third-party neutrals; (2) timing and ripeness; (3) going slow to go fast; (4) providing opportunities for the combatants to get to know and understand one another; (5) the use of a third party BATNA; and (6) flexibility.

1. *The use of third party neutrals* The role played by third-party agencies, such as the UN, in international conflicts, can be critical in reaching agreements. While UN failures to help broker peace agreements have been well publicised in the popular press, the role of the UN in helping to broker peace agreements has not been as well publicised. Among the roles that third-party neutrals can play are to suggest options that neither of the belligerents may have thought of or would have been able to make for political reasons. They can also provide for face-saving where the belligerents do not have to worry about who made the first move and/or concession. Lastly, third-party neutrals can be in a position to influence the participants by 'rewarding' them for moving towards a settlement and 'punishing' them for behaviour that would make settlement less likely.

2. *Timing and ripeness* Shakespeare said, 'Ripeness is all'. Ripeness, in conflict management, means that the conflict is 'ripe' for settlement. There are two conditions that are closely associated with 'ripeness' in conflict-resolution. The first requires that the combatants are equally powerful, i.e., no one combatant has a tactical advantage over the other so that a condition of stalemate exists. The second condition is related to timing. Ripeness in terms of timing means that the combatants have been exhausted by the conflict and wish to reach an agreement. When a conflict is 'ripe', therefore, it is a good time to intervene. Timing and ripeness were critical factors in the Kilometre 101 negotiations because both countries found themselves in a mutually disadvantageous stalemate.

3. *Going slow to go fast* William Ury stated in *Getting Past No* that sometimes one has to know 'When to go slow to go fast'. This means that many negotiations are 'front-end loaded' and will take a significant amount of time – possibly more time than the parties ever imagined. An excellent analogy of the time often required for this type of negotiation is the well-known news story of rescuing 'Baby Jessica' from a well. 'Baby Jessica' was a toddler who accidentally fell into, and subsequently became stuck in, a well. To save her, the rescue team needed to reach her as quickly as possible. However, if they worked too quickly, they could have caused the well to cave in, which would have been equally disastrous. Therefore, the rescuers had to 'Go slow to go fast'. In a similar fashion, the K101 negotiations were built up step by step.

This is not to say that the 'Go slow to go fast' approach should be used in all negotiations. It is more of a rule of thumb, and as such, it is useful approximately 80 per cent of the time. Intuition, based on experience, helps the negotiator to have a good sense of when and when not to apply different tactics.

4. *Providing opportunities for understanding* Integral to this process during the Kilometre 101 negotiations was the opportunity for the Egyptian and Israeli generals to learn about and understand each others' concerns, and get to know each other in different contexts (e.g., as men who loved and missed their families), which helped to break down the traditional stereotypes of each other.

5. *Third-party BATNA* The main issues that had to be negotiated were: how to resupply the cut-off Egyptian Third Army with food and medicine; when and how to exchange POWs; when and how to return normal civilian life to the Canal zone, and how to develop an agreement regarding the disengagement and withdrawal of forces.

Israel took a firm position that they would not allow the Egyptian Third Army to be resupplied with food and medicine until the Israeli POWs were returned. Egypt took a firm stand that the POWs would not be returned until the Third Army was resupplied, which resulted in a deadlock. A great deal of pressure was brought to bear on Israel to soften its position by third parties. One version of what happened is that Dr Kissinger warned Israel that if it did not allow the Egyptian Third Army to be resupplied, the United States would not intervene if the Soviet Union resupplied the Third Army, and this forced the Israelis to be more flexible.

6. *Flexibility* Flexibility and the building of goodwill are crucial to achieving breakthroughs in any negotiation. One side must signal to the other that it is willing to demonstrate some amount of flexibility and goodwill. However, for most negotiations of this type to work, there must be a judicious balance between forcefulness and flexibility. For example, the Egyptians demonstrated their goodwill early in the negotiations by releasing an Israeli POW who had been held for many years in Egypt.

One of the last issues to be negotiated was a model for the disengagement of forces. Standing in the way of the agreement was the Israeli Egyptian disagreement on the withdrawal of Egyptian forces from the East Bank of the Suez Canal. The Israeli position was that there should be no Egyptian troops on the East Bank. The Egyptian position was that it would station its second and third armies on the East Bank.

An agreement had been reached: here would be forces stationed but they would be reduced in number. Because both sides demonstrated flexibility, the agreement was signed for the disengagement of forces. In developing this creative solution, they also developed a mental model of how to use innovation and flexibility that would stand them in good stead in future negotiations.

Collaborative model-building The final element that can help ensure success in the Stage 2 negotiation phase is collaborative model-building. In a seminal article entitled 'Mediating Science-Intensive Policy Disputes', Connie Ozawa and Lawrence Susskind (1985, pp. 33–4) describe three principles that can be used in collaborative model-building to help in resolving intense disputes:

1. Intensive disputes frequently revolve around projections of the likely consequences of proposed actions.
2. If the parties to a technical dispute can develop a model that incorporates key assumptions acceptable to all of them, they are more likely to produce a prediction that none can easily dismiss.
3. Models can be used to facilitate a settlement as long as the model structure is perceived as neutral with respect to the interests of the parties involved.

As computer programs become increasingly sophisticated, they will be used more and more to help to resolve difficult disputes. An illustrative example of collaborative model-building, using advanced computer programs, took place during the Dayton Accord to end the war in Bosnia-Herzegovina. One of the principles that the Serbs and the Bosnians had agreed to was the 51–49 formula, whereby the Bosnians would control 51 per cent of the country and the Serbs would control 49 per cent. Although the formula was easy to agree to in principle, deciding which parcels of land would be Serbian and which would be Bosnian was an extremely difficult matter to negotiate. In his book, *To End a War*, Richard Holbrooke (1998) describes how a sophisticated computer program called PowerScene helped the parties reach an historic agreement.

PowerScene allowed the mediators and the disputants to build a model of all of the land under dispute. By changing the parameters in the program, the parties could try out literally thousands of boundaries and access corridors. The collaborative model-building was instrumental in helping them to reach a settlement.

The above example clearly illustrates the power of model-building, and in particular, computer model-building, in helping to settle disputes. As computer simulations become increasingly sophisticated and the cost of high-end computers and computer programs becomes more affordable, the use of computer-modelling to help settle disputes will increase, giving negotiators and mediators one more tool to help settle intense disputes.

STAGE 3: IMPLEMENTATION

Let us now move on to Stage 3 of Susskind's model: the implementation/post-negotiation phase, which we may represent as follows:

Stage 3: Implementation/post-negotiation

- Monitoring/verification
- Renegotiation: reassembling the participants if subsequent disagreements emerge; helping to remind the parties of their earlier intentions

---

As this book is being written, the UN is monitoring the peace accord in Kosovo. As of 28 June 1999, the Kosovo Liberation Army had to turn in all heavy weapons and stop wearing military uniforms. Further monitoring and renegotiations are also due to take place in order to maintain and enhance the peace arrangements.

THINKING OUTSIDE OF THE BOX

The success of each of the three stages described above often depends on the practitioner's ability to 'think outside of the box'. It is for this reason that this chapter ends with six methods designed to help all of us to think more productively and creatively in order to solve the tasks inherent in each stage of the model.

Innovation, flexibility and 'thinking outside of the box' are important tools for all negotiators and problem-solvers. Fortunately, these are learnable skills. Six methods to help us learn are: (1) processing examples of creative solutions one has arrived at in the past and seeing which elements of those solutions might transfer to a current situation; (2) consulting with other creative thinkers and asking for their assistance; (3) reading about as many creative solutions as possible and making a list of the most creative solutions and/or mental models that were used to arrive at those solutions; (4) processing other examples of creative solutions and following the reasoning backwards to identify the mental model used to generate the creative solution; (5) learning how to use enhanced brainstorming; (6) keeping a creative solutions' log in which you record a description of the creative solutions and/or the mental model used to arrive at the solution, so that the next time you find that you are stuck in a box, you can consult your log. (You will be surprised at how often examples in your log can help you 'think outside of the box'.)

1. *Processing examples of former creative solutions* The next time you get stuck trying to find the answer to a difficult problem, think of examples of previous solutions to other seemingly difficult problems and see if elements of those solutions can be applied to the present situation.

2. *Consulting with other creative thinkers* We all become habituated to looking at a problem in the same way, and sometimes we just can't see our way out of the self-imposed boundaries we place on a particular problem. For example, each of us has lost a set of glasses or keys. We turn the house upside down and can't find the lost item anywhere. We ask another person to have a quick look for us and, within a short period of time, he or she finds the missing item for us. The ability to look at a problem from a fresh perspective is often the key to solving an apparently insoluble problem.

(For example, our school board was in a very difficult financial situation. One way to save money was to hire fewer teachers and/or to increase class sizes. A school board official decided that one way to save money was to have only one grade six class at our school. However, there were eight students over the regulated maximum class limit of 35 students. The school board official's answer was to bus eight students out of our school to another school. As you can imagine, the staff, parents and students were extremely upset, especially the eight students, who could not understand why they had been selected to leave their school and the community that they had been a part of for the entire six years they had been in school. However, after consulting with our school principal, the parents of the students who were being asked to leave the school, the new superintendent and the principal, we found a solution that would combine one of the grade 5 classes and the eight grade 6 students into a split 5/6 class in our school, thereby saving the desired teaching position without forcing eight students away from their school.)

3. *Reading and listing creative solutions and/or the mental models used to achieve them* Many of the books from the Harvard Program on Negotiation contain good examples of creative solutions. Other excellent sources are the books on emotional intelligence by Daniel Goleman (see Reference).

4. *Processing other examples of creative solutions and following the reasoning to identify the mental model* One of the creative solutions that was put forward at the Program for Negotiation for the American League Baseball strike was to have a 'virtual strike'. In a 'virtual strike', the players would continue to play, but would receive only enough money to cover their expenses. Likewise the owners of the ball teams would continue to receive enough money to cover their expenses. A neutral bank would hold all of the extra money. Each day that the players and owners didn't settle, an increasingly large amount of the money that was put in escrow would be turned over to charity. By the time 50 million dollars had been accumulated, half of which was to be turned over to charity, there would be a tremendous amount of pressure on both sides to settle.

One way to learn how to find similar creative solutions in the future is by working backwards to try to figure out how other problem-solvers arrived at the solutions to their problems. As the original situation unfolded, both the players and the owners came to appear more and more greedy to the general public. The opposite of greed is charity. Therefore, the creators of this solution needed to look for a solution that had being charitable at its heart. In other words, how could the negative impression of being greedy be reframed positively? Therefore, reframing negatives into positives is one of the methods that can be used to help invent creative solutions.

5. *Learning how to use enhanced brainstorming* We have all used brainstorming successfully to help us think outside of the box. The ground rules for brainstorming are that we have a set period of time, for example, the next half-hour, to say any idea that comes into our minds with absolutely no criticism. Often an idea that seems ill-conceived may be an innovative solution to a problem, can lead to an innovative idea, or can be combined with other ideas to help resolve a problem. Two innovative procedures that can help enhance the traditional ground-rules of brainstorming are as follows:

First, even though we know the ground-rules, many times we silently criticise someone else's suggestion to ourselves. One way to get around this natural tendency is to ask the other parties involved to come up with different ways to make someone else's suggestion work, rather than to think about ways that it won't work. Once again, no criticism is allowed in the brainstorming process. This procedure helps us use brainstorming not only in the generation of ideas, but also in their implementation.

The second method is a high-tech solution to the problem of some of the parties' ideas being given more or less weight because of who they are or the status they hold. For example, in some parts of the Canadian military they use brainstorming sessions via e-mail. This way, a colonel's ideas are given the same weight as a private's. No one knows whose idea it is, which helps to ensure that all ideas are equally considered.

6. *Keeping a creative solutions' log* People who are good at telling jokes keep a list of materials to draw from. They also practise telling jokes, and learn how to use the right word and the right pause at the right time. Just as joke-telling is a learned art, so is the art of creative problem-solving by learning to 'think outside of the box'. By keeping a creative solutions' log in which you keep a description of the solutions and/or the mental models used to arrive at creative solutions, and consulting it the next time you find that you are stuck in a box, you will be surprised at how often examples in your log can help you think outside of the box. This chapter could be the start of your own creative solutions' log. If you have any examples that you would be willing to share, please mail, fax, or e-mail them to me at my address (see References).

CONCLUSION

Martin Luther King once said: 'People learned to swim like the fish in the water, to fly like birds in the sky. But on earth we still have to learn to live like brothers and sisters.' Judicious use of the above model can help to resolve disputes and so promote the harmony that King dreamed of.

REFERENCES

Bildt, C. (1998), *Peace Journey: The Struggle for Peace in Bosnia* (London: Weidenfeld & Nicolson).
Goleman, D. (1995), *Emotional Intelligence* (New York: Bantam Books).
—— (1998), *Working with Emotional Intelligence* (New York: Bantam Books).
Holbrooke, R. (1998), *To End a War* (New York: Random House).
MacKenzie, L. (1993), *Peacekeeper: The Road to Sarajevo* (Vancouver: Douglas & McIntyre).
McRae, B., can be contacted at 5880 Spring Garden Road, Suite 400, Halifax, NS, CANADA, B3H 1Y1, Telephone (902) 423-4680, Fax (902) 492-2330. E-mail *bmcrae@ns.sympatico.ca* Website *www3.ns.sympatico.ca/bmcrae*.
Ozawa, C.P. and Susskind, L. (1985), 'Mediating Science-Intensive Policy Disputes', *Journal of Policy Analysis and Management*, 5: 1, pp. 23–39.
Susskind, L. and Cruickshank J. (1988), *Breaking the Impasse: Consensual Approaches to Resolving Public Disputes* (New York: Basic Books).

PART 2
Negotiation and the Military

4

The Anatomy of Conditionality and Linkage: Negotiating for Life[1]

STUART GORDON

Between 1992 and 1995 the UN Security Council passed 89 resolutions relating to the conflict in Bosnia-Herzegovina. These ultimately led the UN Protection Force (UNPROFOR) into a mandate that was logically absurd: it was forced to make war and peace, to bomb and to support the feeding of the same people, at the same time and on the same territory.[2]

The ineffectual, and some would argue counterproductive, UN military deployment can be seen in the context of an enormous endeavour by UN and non-governmental humanitarian organisations (NGOs) to ameliorate the suffering created by the wars throughout Former Yugoslavia. In 1994 UNHCR/DHA estimates suggest that nearly 3 million people were beneficiaries of direct emergency relief aid.[3] The UN High Commission for Refugees (UNHCR), the UN's lead agency in Former Yugoslavia, facilitated the delivery of over 950,000 metric tonnes of humanitarian assistance. It became the UNHCR's largest humanitarian operation up until that point.[4]

However, the UNHCR, through its negotiations, often failed to secure access to beleaguered populations, and their agreements with the belligerents did not always reflect humanitarian 'needs'. This chapter explores why this occurred through an examination of the impact of UNHCR's coordination mechanisms on its relations with the Bosnian Serbs, the phenomenon and causes of 'linkage' and the problems generated by the Sarajevo airport agreement.

THE HUMANITARIAN CATASTROPHE

The war had a catastrophic and tragic impact upon the people of Bosnia, an impact which went far beyond the immediate pain and suffering of the individual. Massive population transfers, both as a consequence and as a means of war ensured that the economic, political and social viability of a multiethnic state of Bosnia-Herzegovina was destroyed.

Populations, mobilised along ethnic lines, viewed the existence of other ethnic groups as a threat to their own existence. This served to widen the cast of combatants and 'legitimate' targets – civilians, economic infrastructure, public utilities and aid workers serving and sustaining 'enemy' communities – that contemporary international humanitarian law proscribes. Thus ethnic war simultaneously served as the motive for broad intercommunal violence and the means through which adherence to Western norms of war was undermined.

The destruction of the economic infrastructure and the movement of people displaced by the violence created an enormous, multidimensional and immediate humanitarian catastrophe. This was exacerbated by the relatively high levels of economic development in prewar Bosnia-Herzegovina which, perhaps paradoxically, served to reduce the population's capacity to withstand the economic effects of war.[5] Duffield argues that their almost complete prewar reliance upon paid employment and regional/national utility networks ensured that the war caused an almost complete dislocation of prewar social and economic structures.[6]

The resulting economic and social disruption created circumstances that enabled local civil and military commanders to use the war effort for personal as well as political gain. War and humanitarian assistance therefore also provided the means through which personal enrichment and aggrandisement could be achieved, often through direct collusion with the leaders of ethnic groups across the confrontation lines. For example, members of the Croat population of Mostar frequently traded food with the besieged Muslims while the Krajina Serbs routinely traded both with the Muslim forces loyal to the rebel Muslim, Fikret Abdic, and to the Sarajevo government's own 5th Corps trapped in the Bihac pocket. The 'privatisation' of national and local economies also marginalised individuals, contributing to the rise of individual and collective banditry. Predations on the civilians and the humanitarian community were but one of the results. Their misery, therefore, had several dimensions to it.

Before the war the population of the former Yugoslavia was largely dependent on government-run public utility networks (gas and water pipelines, electricity grids, etc.), which served entire regions rather than single ethnic populations. During Bosnia-Herzegovina's war this dependence introduced what Duffield describes as 'utility politics'.[7] Populations which controlled the top of a distribution network could withhold supplies in order to extract concessions from populations at the bottom. These arrangements could be broken down through bargaining based upon immovable humanitarian principles such as the right to deliver food on the basis of 'needs'. Nevertheless, the resultant deals often enmeshed humanitarian agencies and their programmes in arrangements which linked access to food and public utilities for one community to benefits to another. This was part of a general pattern of obstructionism perpetrated by all three belligerents.

To some extent the Bosnian Serbs felt particularly justified in obstructing humanitarian assistance to Croat and Muslim communities as a consequence of their, not entirely inaccurate, perception that the international humanitarian effort was biased against them. The majority of humanitarian agencies worked largely in Muslim- and Croat-controlled areas – a fact which also reflected the obstructionism of the Bosnian Serbs and the desperate 'human needs' in Muslim and Croat areas. However, it also resulted from the unpopularity of Serb populated areas with donor governments[8] as well as the focus of international sanctions. The result of these perceptions was that obstructionism became a persistent and generalised feature of the Bosnian war. In such a context a coordinated humanitarian response was essential.

COORDINATING HUMANITARIAN RESPONSES – GENERIC ISSUES

While most humanitarian agencies agree that coordinating their efforts is good in principle, few UN agencies or NGOs prove to be active supporters of the principle in practice. Allowing one's agency to become sub-ordinated within a broad 'humanitarian effort' may have adverse implications in terms of public profile and funding. Furthermore, 'turf battles', particularly between UN agencies, often preclude genuine coordination.[9] Nevertheless, functional 'coordination' may emerge naturally, particularly among NGOs, as a consequence of what could be described as 'humanitarian pull'. For example, in the health sector functional pressures may force coordination upon NGOs. The problems of communicable diseases in mass population migrations and refugee camps ensure that an integrated approach between medical and sanitation NGOs is often essential. Similarly, coordination may become necessary in order to present a united front to armed factions. This may create enough pressure to persuade them to comply with acceptable codes of behaviour. Van Brabant provides an example of this drawn from the experiences of NGOs operating in Liberia's capital, Monrovia, during 1994. He describes how all of the UN store-houses had been looted and the remaining NGOs coordinated their meetings with factional leaders in order to present a united front.[10] Hence, coordination may emerge for a variety of reasons: for example, as a means of improving the security environment or as a mechanism for reducing costs and improving efficiency by avoiding the duplication of effort, and responding to emergencies for which one agency is not sufficiently equipped or experienced. Nevertheless, pressures mitigating against coordination are at least as strong as 'functional pull', particularly in an acute, complex emergency. UN agencies and NGOs compete, to a degree, for funding and profile among their peers. Hence, subordinating their priorities and profile within a coordination mechanism dominated by another agency may be an option with few incentives. In the case of the humanitarian response to the crisis in Bosnia the UN adopted a coordination mechanism known as the lead agency concept with the UN High Commissioner for Refugees adopting the lead.

UNHCR'S LEAD AGENCY ROLE

UNHCR was invited to assume this role largely because of its experience in the management of refugee populations and its relative capacity (in comparison with other UN agencies) within the region. Pugh identifies its particular institutional strengths. By 1993 it had a budget of $1,127 billion, assisted some 18 million refugees world wide[11] and had a greater presence in the Balkans than any other potential UN 'lead agency' rival. Minear *et al.* also identify that by the end of 1993 there were over 700 international and local staff, 29 offices and a budget appeal figure in excess of $295 million.[12]

As lead agency UNHCR viewed its role as that of coordinating the activities of all other UN humanitarian agencies and accredited NGOs. Yet the mechanisms for ensuring coordination ensured that a blurring of institutional lines occurred among the humanitarian agencies and also with UNPROFOR. This ultimately had damaging consequences for UNHCR's relationships with the Bosnian Serbs and the nature of subsequent negotiations.

The lead agency concept was also resented by staff from other humanitarian agencies. While most recognised the need for a 'coordinated response', resentments arose partly from the fact that it placed one agency in a position of authority over others and partly because it frequently generated responsibilities for which the appointed lead agency often had little appropriate experience. By the time that UNHCR assumed the role in Bosnia the concept itself was also somewhat anachronistic. The performance of UN humanitarian agencies during the Kurdish exodus following the second Gulf War had led to the creation[13] of a new set of mechanisms for ensuring the coordination of humanitarian assistance: principally, the Department of Humanitarian Affairs (DHA) headed by a new Emergency Relief Coordinator[14] and an Inter-Agency Standing Committee, chaired by the Emergency Relief Coordinator (ERC) and comprising UN agencies, the ICRC and key NGOs. In effect, the new strategic coordination mechanism removed the need for a specialist agency to exercise the degree of control over its peers that the lead agency concept could potentially imply.

Pugh identifies that these new mechanisms proved to be of little use in the response to the humanitarian catastrophe which befell Yugoslavia from 1991.[15] Essentially, the UN humanitarian agencies were confronted by the crisis in Former Yugoslavia *before* the lessons of the Gulf emergency had been absorbed and the necessary reorganisation effected.[16] Consequently, the UN Secretariat had to rely on existing mechanisms to manage humanitarian coordination.

In 1992 UNHCR faced more than 40 NGOs wishing to provide services to Bosnians affected by the fighting.[17] The NGOs involved throughout this period were exceptionally diverse in terms of a range of factors: size, sources of funding, operating principles, capacities, competencies and so on. The diversity obviously presented challenges for any coordinating structure. Furthermore, the operating mandates of some NGOs presented insuperable difficulties for any mechanism. For example, those NGOs who viewed their mandates as simply or largely providing a human rights advocacy function were difficult to include in any operational coordinating mechanism. Similarly, some NGOs effectively took sides in the conflict by working only with one community.[18] For example, various national Red Crescent societies, in particular the Iranian Red Crescent and Mahomet groups, supported only Muslim populations in Bosnia. Save the Children Fund (Croatia) worked only in Croat-controlled Prozor and refused to employ Muslims in several school and education projects even after the 23 February 1994 ceasefire. CARITAS (a Catholic NGO operating from Croatia) also tended to work largely in Croat-controlled areas, while Dobrotvor (an Orthodox NGO working from Serbia) tended to work in Serb-controlled regions. Yet others, ICRC and MSF for example, fearing embroilment in the crisis itself through over-association with UNPROFOR and/or UNHCR, were unwilling to be seen to coordinate too closely with UNHCR for fear that it would prejudice their independence and, consequently, their ability to operate among all communities. As the security situation deteriorated in 1993 and the UN Security Council, at least in declaratory terms, began to provide UNPROFOR with an increasingly robust mandate, many other NGOs also became concerned that they would be perceived to be associated with UNHCR (as lead agency) which was itself dependent upon an increasingly belligerent UNPROFOR. In such a context they could maintain perceptions of their independence only through limiting contact with UNHCR and UNPROFOR units, or bypassing them altogether. However, the security situation and a general paucity of funding made such an option increasingly difficult.

UNHCR's coordination role was also complicated by other factors. Certainly in the first 12 months of the emergency phase UNHCR adopted a very positive form of management, in preference to a more light-handed touch, designed to *facilitate* rather than *direct* the work of other agencies in accordance with their own particular mandates. In part this reflected the nature of a logistics operation routinely obstructed by the belligerents and suffering from a general lack of capacity in the face of enormous demands for (principally) food and equipment for the coming winter. Consequently, logistics priorities generally did not allow for much flexibility in terms of carrying non-food items. For some agencies this led to a degree of frustration with UNHCR. This resentment was also felt in terms of UNHCR's attempts to maintain direct operational control across a range of emergency relief activities which extended beyond its own mandate, perceived competencies and even resources. This resentment was translated into other UN agencies investing less in responding to the crisis than perhaps they would otherwise have done.[19]

Furthermore, the obvious difficulties involved in pursuing an active 'protection' strategy in the face of ethnic cleansing (and given the absence of international military enforcement action) ensured that the humanitarian programme was defined largely in terms of logistics. This had the effect of 'crowding out' elements of the non-food humanitarian agenda[20] and generated controversies, even within UNHCR, as to the degree to which its 'protection' mandate had been eclipsed. This was made more striking by accusations from a wide variety of sources that it was failing to provide sufficient 'protection' to the internally displaced and those in danger within their own homes. Pugh,[21] for example, identifies that UNHCR's strategies for providing protection in Bosnia emphasised regional and 'in-country' solutions largely in deference to Western donors' preferences to limit immigration to or asylum in the West. However, in the face of ethnic cleansing UNHCR lacked the staff, resources and even the level of access to the beleaguered communities which was necessary to provide even a rudimentary form of protection (or even to rule on whether evacuation or remaining *in situ* constituted appropriate responses), and opened UNHCR to the criticism that it had failed in its increasing responsibilities to the internally displaced.

Criticisms that UNHCR lacked the resources or experience to deal effectively with the range of its tasks were compounded by its assumption of responsibilities for infrastructure repair and a degree of economic rehabilitation. Thus, on the initiative of the UNHCR, an International Management Group Infrastructure for Bosnia and Herzegovina (IMG-BH) was formally established by donor governments in November 1994. This was created in order both to address the infrastructure needs of Bosnia-Herzegovina and to 'bridge the gap between emergency relief activities and reconstruction in anticipation that refugees would return'.[22] This led to something of a dilemma for UNHCR: while a 'holistic' approach appeared desirable in principle, it led to UNHCR spreading its capacities too thinly and engendered a further overstretch of UNHCR's 'competence'. The reconstruction of federation infrastructure without similar programmes in Bosnian Serb territory also brought UNHCR's 'impartiality' into question.[23]

COORDINATING THE NGOS: THE PRINCIPLES[24]

Active emergency relief NGO coordination throughout central Bosnia-Herzegovina between 1992 and 1995 was effected essentially through accreditation with UNHCR. Duffield[25] argues that accreditation could be obtained through acceptance of the UNHCR's principles of association: negotiated access, coordination and protection. In a practical sense nearly all NGOs working inside Bosnia depended to some extent upon UNHCR, in particular for the security afforded by UNPROFOR (available, nominally at least, only to UNHCR-accredited NGOs). The exceptions were limited to ICRC (as a consequence of its operating principles) and those few organisations that tended to work only with one community.

Association with UNHCR was, in essence, a bargain between UNHCR and the NGO. Accreditation ensured that NGOs were given access to UNHCR logistical and transport resources, UNHCR identity cards, Bosnian vehicle-registration plates, and programme support and funding, as well as UNPROFOR protection for convoys. Accreditation was also intended by UNHCR to provide 'legitimacy' (in the eyes of the belligerents) for the non-UN relief effort. It also purposefully linked the UN, NGO and governmental relief efforts. From 1991 UNHCR deliberately endeavoured to blur the distinction between UN agencies and the NGOs in order to encourage the belligerents to treat all humanitarian organisations equally and to ensure their easy identification on the battlefield and respect for their humanitarian status.[26] It was also hoped that this would improve the chances of NGOs gaining access to people in need.[27] Furthermore, this conflation of the humanitarian community was exacerbated by UNHCR in the course of negotiations with the belligerents through UNHCR representing both itself and the wider 'humanitarian community'. In return for accreditation UNHCR was furnished with reports on programmes and was able to exercise a degree of coordination and active management of a diverse set of emergency-related activities. Hence, accreditation could be seen as an exchange of services.

THE PRICE OF ACCREDITATION

The conflation of all of the elements of the humanitarian community, resulting both from UNHCR's interpretation of its lead agency role and the nature of the accreditation bargain, generated both positive and negative results. Cutts suggests that the popularity of the UN identity cards and vehicle-registration plates among the NGO community suggests that it served positively to improve humanitarian access and to overcome some of the attempts by the belligerents to differentiate between the different types of humanitarian organisation. He argues that by the end of 1995 this resulted in some 3,000 individuals, representing over 250 humanitarian organisations, carrying UNHCR identity documents.

Nevertheless, this improvement in general access was bought at a price felt in terms of UNHCR's own credibility and, therefore, its own ease of access. On the occasions when less professional NGOs and non-humanitarian holders of identity cards abused the system it 'had the unfortunate effect of tarring UNHCR with the same brush'.[28] Cutts identifies that identity cards and vehicle-registration plates were, at times, issued without sufficient attention being invested in differentiating bona fide humanitarian staff from others. In fairness to UNHCR, Bosnia attracted new and sometimes ephemeral (and, at times, less than competent) NGOs and the provision of UN documentation to such groups served to discredit the humanitarian effort only in a limited way. However, inadvertently issuing cards to Cutts' list[29] of undercover journalists, to human rights activists posing as humanitarian staff, to limited numbers of embassy staff, and even to some ambassadors brought the system into a degree of discredit among those manning the checkpoints through which humanitarian convoys passed. This was compounded by the fact that UN identity cards routinely and easily entered the black market, where they were obtained by Bosnian civilians who used them as a means of getting through checkpoints and escaping from the country. Bosnian civilians also routinely applied for work in humanitarian organisations, again in order to obtain UN identity cards. Consequently, as a means of escape, identity cards had value in the black economy of Bosnia but brought a small but cumulative degree of discredit to the collective humanitarian effort.

The conflation of the various humanitarian agencies was also accentuated by their use of UNHCR registration plates and stickers for their vehicles. Consequently, UNHCR and NGO vehicles often looked identical. Cutts points out that by August 1995 there were over 2,000 vehicles from more than 150 humanitarian organisations fitted with UNHCR registration plates. Just as with the identity cards for individuals, this system was also abused. Sometimes these vehicles were used to smuggle commercial goods across front-lines. At times, the belligerents 'spiced' such accusations with suggestions that these vehicles were running arms and ammunition to their opponents.

NEGOTIATED ACCESS

Despite the (often unimplementable)[30] enforcement provisions of UNPROFOR's mandate, UNHCR maintained access to beleaguered populations through negotiations with and the consent of the local factions. One component of the accreditation bargain was an effort to restrict the number of organisations authorised to negotiate with the belligerent factions.[31] Consequently, UNHCR attempted to ensure that only its own senior staff negotiated access agreements with the belligerent factions. These agreements were then distributed to all NGOs, regardless of whether or not they were accredited. Such a regime also provided a mechanism for passively coordinating the humanitarian effort as well as encouraging perceptions that the international humanitarian aid and UNHCR's own efforts were synonymous.

COORDINATION AND SECURITY

The main coordination tool available to the UNHCR was administrative: the monthly plan. This plan was a compilation of needs assessments, projected relief needs and detailed convoy movements, and was forwarded not only to the belligerents (a routine measure with negotiated access agreements) but also to all NGOs, regardless of whether or not they were accredited. Accredited agencies identified their own transport requirements in consultation with the UNHCR needs assessment. UNHCR sub-offices then coordinated the consolidated transport requirements with UNPROFOR and local civic/military authorities in order to provide both security and access. UNPROFOR advised on the safety of the chosen route, the security requirements and also, sometimes, negotiated access with local factions (using the military liaison officer network)[32] and provided additional transport where necessary and when available.

The monthly plan worked reasonably well, despite the systematic obstructionism of local belligerent commanders, until October 1993 when the Bosnian Croat and then the Bosnian Serb authorities insisted on the weekly identification of movements. As a mechanism designed to obstruct movements this worked extremely well, leading bilateral donor governments and the UN High Commissioner for Refugees herself to insist, in November 1993, that all of the belligerents should provide access agreements based on acceptance of a needs-based approach.

The monthly plan was an apparently passive coordination tool in that it was a means of dispensing information and, through this, avoiding duplication of effort. However, in the sense that inclusion of NGO programmes within this document was the key to receiving UNPROFOR convoy protection and acceptance by factions, it also contained elements of an 'active' coordination mechanism.

NGO DEPENDENCY UPON UNHCR

The number of NGOs operating within Bosnia increased throughout 1993 and significantly again after the signing of the Croat–Muslim Washington Peace Accords in February 1994. Duffield[33] suggests that most were concentrated in the more stable and less politically sensitive areas in Central Bosnia and few ventured into the most dangerous or into Serb-controlled territory.

The majority of larger NGOs voluntarily accepted the requirement for a coordinating body. The relationship between UNHCR and these NGOs was conditioned upon 'consent' in the sense that they agreed to participate in the operational priority-setting functions of UNHCR providing that their own institutional mandates were represented. For smaller NGOs there was often a conscious effort to secure what were, in effect, UNHCR humanitarian subcontracts. UNHCR, lacking institutional capacity and a standing mandate, sought to subcontract many humanitarian functions that went beyond its own institutional core competencies. This ensured that any comparative advantage an NGO may have had contributed to the increased effectiveness of the UNHCR coordinated effort. It also helped to reduce the impact of the UNHCR's lack of staff. Nevertheless, it did serve further to conflate the different types of humanitarian response in the eyes of Bosnia's belligerent parties. It also contributed to what could be described as a rather generalised systemic dependence of NGOs upon UNHCR.

One of the pillars of this dependence, identified by Mark Duffield,[34] was a general lack of alternative funding sources for NGOs. The combined EC/EU and bilateral aid programmes amounted to some 65 per cent of all aid to Former Yugoslavia.[35] Yet bilateral donor agencies were increasingly becoming involved operationally, both directly and in terms of influencing the operational priorities of the NGOs which they funded. A part of this 'operationalisation' was increasingly to use UNPROFOR troops as conduits through which emergency assistance projects could be implemented. Such changes represented a response both to perceived political pressure from donor governments for greater visibility and also to dissatisfaction with the implementing capacities of the NGO community.[36] However, the result was to limit the sources of funding for NGOs operating within Bosnia. Duffield identifies the impact of this phenomenon most starkly in his figures relating to the British Overseas Development Administration's financial year 1992/93 budget. He points out that less than 6 per cent of the £73 million budget for Former Yugoslavia was provided through NGOs.[37]

Limiting the sources of funding served to increase the dependence upon UNHCR funding of those NGOs without alternative means of raising funds, thereby increasing pressure upon them to seek accreditation to UNHCR and also bringing them into direct competition with UNPROFOR units. The key point, however, is that NGOs, the UN humanitarian agencies and UNPROFOR appeared to the belligerents to be becoming increasingly 'integrated'. Furthermore, UNHCR's obviously close association with UNPROFOR, and UNPROFOR's increasingly belligerent stance towards the Bosnian Serbs, served to erode much of the remaining humanitarian space.

WHY CONTROL?

Perhaps the key problem for UNHCR as the lead agency was, however, to determine the degree to which NGO freedom was desirable and/or inevitable in an operation which lacked a centralised state authority and was becoming increasingly dependent upon military protection. The costs of failing to coordinate were, potentially, serious. For example, repetition of needs assessments, and therefore of relief deliveries, could have had a profound impact not only upon the recipients, in terms of their ability to withstand siege and provide food to troops, but also upon the communities which, as a consequence, did not receive the aid. The reactions of the belligerents would also have been affected. Furthermore, within the first year of the Bosnian relief operation, UNHCR and UNPROFOR found that as a result of the profusion of fairly independent humanitarian agencies the negotiations with local civil and military leaderships regarding various humanitarian issues were conducted in a highly uncoordinated fashion. In an environment where manipulation of the humanitarian agencies was frequent, this led to considerable problems.

The uncoordinated efforts and, more importantly, the unconventional practice allegedly used by some NGOs could destroy entire networks of trust. The 'networks of trust' ensured the passage of convoys through particular checkpoints on a regular basis. For example, in background briefings several UN military observers[38] claimed that in 1992–93 staff from one British *ad hoc* NGO routinely attempted to smuggle explosives into Sarajevo on falsified UNHCR documentation. The explosives were the charges for detonating caps, to be used to mine for coal in order to provide domestic heating fuel for the population of Sarajevo, but discovery by the Serbs would have lead to increased obstructionism in future.

Part of this problem related to what some UNPROFOR and UNHCR officers suggested were the rather limited horizons of some of the smaller, often *ad hoc*,[39] non-accredited agencies. Certainly, the larger NGOs felt that for some of these ephemeral groups the passage of their one convoy was viewed in isolation from the broader aid effort. (This contrasted with the perceptions of the larger NGOs which predicted that their involvement would last beyond that of UNPROFOR.) As a consequence, the *ad hoc* agencies were frequently unaware of the regimes governing the basis upon which aid was distributed. Providing aid outside of these regimes and strategic frameworks risked both manipulation by the warring factions and compromising relationships necessary to sustain large-scale operations rather than single transactions. In effect, every effort was made to feed communities on either side of a confrontation line on the basis of 'need' rather than on formulae relating to populations. Thus a subtle 'packaging' of bargains was required to avoid the appearance of linkage.

In the absence of an embracing host government–UNHCR agreement specifying the humanitarian strategy and hierarchy, and with the financial independence of some of the non-accredited NGOs, other means for establishing UNHCR authority, however limited, needed to be created. In Bosnia, a degree of UNHCR authority could be exerted as a result of UNHCR's control of security provision[40] (even to non-accredited NGOs) and reliance upon its in-theatre needs assessment and distribution infrastructure as well as its control of the vehicle-registration procedure. Nevertheless, while UNHCR's ability to control other humanitarian agencies was significant, it was not 'complete'. UNHCR was not a governmental authority with control of state borders. Consequently, individuals and NGOs who refused convoy escorts could still negotiate their own passage into Bosnia-Herzegovina and towards besieged areas. These negotiations could still have a detrimental impact upon the politically sensitive nature of the operation as a whole.

THE PROBLEMS OF AID DELIVERY:
LINKAGE AND CONDITIONALITY

While overt obstructionism of aid and the delivery of essential utilities was commonplace, by far the greatest problem was that of 'linked' or 'conditional' deals which did not reflect humanitarian 'needs' but the 'power' of one party over another. While humanitarian organisations endeavoured to deliver emergency relief aid on the basis of need, warring factions frequently only allowed the distribution of food aid to their, or their opposition's, civilian community if other demands or aspirations were acceded to. This principle was referred to by a number of labels: 'conditionality', 'linkage' and 'reciprocity' being among the most common.

Parties would frequently only agree to humanitarian action, which humanitarian law obligated them to undertake, upon reciprocal action or concessions by their foes. Consequently, an acceptance of a deal made on that basis had a direct impact upon the humanitarian's perceived impartiality and neutrality: the humanitarian was viewed as either for or against the faction that had been conceded to. Such arrangements, if accepted, served to undermine much of what was left of the neutral 'humanitarian space'.

Officially, UNHCR did not accept such 'reciprocity', but stressed that aid would be distributed purely on the basis of need. However, UNHCR found that there was often no other way of keeping the humanitarian operation going, since its continuation depended on the consent of the warring parties, who generally did not accept principles other than those based on assistance proportional to population figures. Consequently, as the war continued, UNHCR increasingly came to accept and practise dilute forms of reciprocity. For example, in response to consistent attempts by the Bosnian Serbs to block deliveries to the besieged government enclaves of Srebrenica, Zepa and Gorazde, UNHCR scheduled deliveries for the enclaves at the beginning of each week and deliveries for the surrounding Serb areas at the end of each week. In this way, when the Bosnian Serbs prevented convoys from entering the enclaves, the subsequent convoys for the civilian population in areas controlled by Bosnian Serb forces were also delayed or suspended. The same tactics were applied during the (multiple and concentric) sieges of Vitez. The food allocation for the town was distributed according to strict formulae for the two besieged enclaves. These formulae were related to population size but, given that both the Croat and Muslim communities were besieged, were clearly also needs-based. The UNHCR policy was all or nothing, if aid was blocked to one community it would be blocked to all. However, such a policy was not immune to the counter-responses of mayors. In conditions where one community was more desperate than another, cutting off one's own supplies made sense, even though both populations suffered. Similarly, one could trade short-term suffering for longer-term gain. For example, in February 1994 the mayor of Novi Travnik blocked the passage of aid into his area until the UNHCR made arrangements for water supplies to be reintroduced.

However, the use and acceptance of linkage by UNPROFOR or any of the UN humanitarian agencies also had the potential for unforeseen negative effects, serving to halt the entire humanitarian effort.[41] Linkages potentially tied the continuity of humanitarian programmes to matters beyond the direct control of the humanitarian agencies, leading to a freezing of negotiations.[42] In circumstances where Security Council resolutions were increasingly placing UNPROFOR in direct conflict with the Bosnian Serbs, linking humanitarian 'progress' to progress on other issues controlled by other factions, or even by UNPROFOR, served to draw UNHCR out of its humanitarian space and weaken its moral authority in negotiations with the increasingly isolated Bosnian Serbs through undermining the consent for or acceptance of (among the belligerent factions) humanitarian principles. It therefore began to erode the humanitarian access regimes through subordinating humanitarian action to political objectives and by undermining the 'acceptability and thus the security of independent and neutral humanitarian action'.[43]

This could also be undermined by the humanitarian staff themselves.

For example, widespread[44] attempts by all sorts of humanitarian staff to deceive or to smuggle aid, private goods, fuel and even journalists past the 'morally bankrupt' belligerents, if discovered, complicated subsequent negotiations over access. Losing the moral high-ground ensured that appeals to lofty humanitarian moral principles rang hollow. The policy of attempting to portray all humanitarian activity as the same (through common identity cards and vehicle-registration plates) also ensured that UNHCR was seen as complicit in and even responsible for the activities of all humanitarian agencies. However, the humanitarian community was not solely responsible. UNPROFOR units in Sarajevo were involved in the trade and passage of black-market goods, smuggled local Bosnian and Bosnian Serb civilians[45] across checkpoints, and even traded their own weapons.[46] Ukrainian troops in Gorazde were also heavily involved in black-market activities during 1995. However, the key point is that appeals to humanitarian principles could not work if they were diluted by acts which broke other 'moral' or 'legal' frames of reference. 'Purity' appeared to be a precondition for moral appeals in the course of negotiations over humanitarian access.

Linkage also proved to be self-perpetuating, contributing to what could be termed as 'humanitarian inflation'. For example, British troops throughout the period between November 1992 (from their initial deployment to Bosnia) and February 1994 (the signing of the Washington Peace Accords) engaged in negotiating civilian prisoner exchanges, frequently in cooperation with the ICRC.[47] The threats of reciprocated executions were sufficient, in the minds of successive battalion commanders, to justify involvement in linked releases.[48] However, while such tactics were successful in the short term, they clearly encouraged repetitions of the same and increases in the prices extracted for releases.

Obstructionism, while enduring, could also take a variety of forms, but perhaps the most surprising was that of self-denial. This provided a useful form of protest and offered 'leverage' to the besieged. For example, in February 1993 the city council of Sarajevo instituted an aid boycott in protest at Serb actions around Sarajevo and Srebrenica. UNHCR temporarily suspended its operations in protest at the apparent politicisation of aid as well as the level of insecurity endured by its staff.[49] Similarly, in March 1994 the Muslim mayors of Maglai and Gorazde obstructed the movement of aid into their towns. In the case of Maglai this appeared to be a local measure designed to place pressure on BSA units to lift the siege.[50] The measures in the case of Gorazde were part of a far more ambitious strategy. Increasing the plight of the besieged population extended even to Muslim government units who deliberately collapsed their own front-lines the following month, in order to draw

Bosnian Serb tanks into the UNPROFOR-defined 'safe area' and thus precipitate NATO airstrikes.[51]

Self-inflicted obstructionism also arose from the very logic of war. For example, besieged communities such as those of Kiseljack, Stari Vitez and Vitez in Central Bosnia, when having to choose between military and humanitarian imperatives, would frequently be forced to allow the former to prevail. Humanitarian convoys could hide the advance of enemy troops or bring civilian populations into exposed and vulnerable positions, while those passing through your territory could also carry weapons to your opponents. In such circumstances, it could be easier to go hungry than to expose civilians and soldiers to such dangers.[52]

While these kinds of argument were used frequently to justify obstructionism of all types, it was clear that they constituted only a small number of the entries in a broad vocabulary of excuses for obstructing aid. It was also clear that UNHCR staff would not sufficiently challenge those responsible for such arguments when they were inappropriate or untrue. Having developed relationships with local power-brokers, particularly in dangerous and volatile environments or where the humanitarian staff were dependent upon those same power-brokers for their own safety, staff would, perhaps understandably, be reluctant to challenge the motivations and decisions of those who obstructed humanitarian efforts. The routine duplicity of local officials in Bosnia made this a critical, albeit understandable, institutional failing on the part of UNHCR.[53]

Nevertheless, UNHCR had only limited tools with which to combat linkage. Consistently, its policy was for officials to pressure all factions to agree that UNHCR and ICRC should be allowed to determine 'without any conditionality or linkages, what humanitarian assistance was needed and where'.[54] They also sought agreement that the 'current cumbersome and frequently deliberately obstructive clearance procedures' should be 'radically simplified immediately'. Despite the belligerents acceptance of these measures in two, much broader agreements on 18 and 29 November 1993, UNHCR found that there was minimal implementation by the warring factions[55] and access remained difficult.[56] This widespread and deliberate bureaucratic and checkpoint obstruction certainly continued with the eastern enclaves until their fall (in the case of Srebrenica and Zepa).

'Linkage' and obstructionism were not simply the *ad hoc* tactics of checkpoint commanders. They could also be major features of agreements reached at the highest levels. The Sarajevo airport agreement, arguably the most flawed, essential and unavoidable of the agreements relating to humanitarian access, was one such agreement.

THE SARAJEVO AIRPORT AGREEMENT

The Sarajevo airport agreement, or 'Agreement of 5 June 1992 on the Re-Opening of Sarajevo Airport for Humanitarian Purposes', was negotiated between UNPROFOR negotiators,[57] the Bosnian Serb authorities and the Bosnian government.[58] UNHCR was not directly represented, and the resultant agreement does not even specifically mention UNHCR. It was an agreement designed to ensure that humanitarian assistance reached the besieged population of Sarajevo, whose plight was becoming increasingly desperate. It enabled the continuation of the Sarajevo airlift, an operation that ultimately rivalled the Berlin airlift and, arguably, in purely technical terms, represented UNHCR's greatest logistical achievement.[59] Some 20 states were involved in the provision of aircraft and technical support to the programme, which lasted from 3 July 1992 until 9 January 1996.

The airlift also represents a tremendous feat of bravery and perseverance. Both the Sarajevo authorities and the Bosnian Serb military routinely endeavoured to frustrate the operation through bureaucratic and military means. While the worst incident was the shooting down of an Italian aircraft, there were over 300 cases of attacks on aircraft using the airport.[60] These incidents often resulted in demands by aircraft-contributing nations for written security guarantees from the belligerents. Their frequent inability to provide these also served as pretexts for ensuring that operations remained suspended.

While the opening of the airport highlighted the bravery of the aircrews and UNHCR staff engaged in the airlift, the agreement itself contained a variety of fundamental flaws, with a range of unintended consequences for the aid programme as a whole. Nevertheless, its failings should be seen in the context of the military situation that prevailed when it was negotiated. The Bosnian Serb army besieged the city of Sarajevo and held the military advantage. As a result of divisions within the UN Security Council[61] the international response appeared to substitute a programme of humanitarian assistance for the type of enforcement action used against Iraq in 1991.[62] Furthermore, as a consequence of ethnic cleansing in Croatia and the brutal sieges of Vukovar and Dubrovnik, the Bosnian Serbs had already been vilified by the international press and were subject to a range of international sanctions. Their pariah status ensured that little additional leverage could be applied. As the humanitarian situation in Sarajevo became increasingly desperate, so, too, did UNPROFOR's negotiations on access to Sarajevo airport. This amounted to an extremely poor negotiating position and was ultimately reflected in the terms of the agreement itself. Consequently,

UNPROFOR had little choice but to agree to a series of concessions in exchange for an amelioration of the increasingly dreadful conditions in Sarajevo.

The problems were twofold. First, the airport agreement allowed for the creation of additional mechanisms for obstructing the passage of aid through the airport. Second, it changed the basis upon which aid was provided from one of an impartial assessment of 'needs' to one based upon what could be described as 'reciprocity' or 'equivalence'.

The first of these problems was caused by the somewhat unintended provision for both belligerents to establish inspectors at the airport in order to facilitate UNPROFOR's control of 'incoming personnel, aid, cargo and other items'.[63] This enabled the Bosnian Serbs bureaucratically to obstruct the delivery of humanitarian assistance without the potential costs, in terms of possible enforcement action, likely to be incurred from a more robust and overt strategy of checkpoint obstructionism. The agreement also made provision for UNPROFOR to establish 'security corridors' between the airport and the city, potentially providing UNPROFOR with a means of overriding decisions made by the airport inspectors. Consequently, the Bosnian Serbs established a heavily defended checkpoint between the airport and the city itself, enabling them, if necessary, to prevent UNPROFOR overriding decisions made by Bosnian Serb airport inspectors.[64] It also severely constrained the ability of UNHCR to move civilians safely across the confrontation line, thereby also limiting an element of its 'protection' function.

The second concession, made in Article 8 of the agreement, was perhaps more serious. It altered the basis upon which humanitarian assistance was delivered and perceived by the belligerents as well as serving to extend their control over other aspects of the humanitarian programme. Article 8 stated that 'humanitarian aid will be delivered to Sarajevo and beyond, under the supervision of the United Nations, in a non-discriminatory manner and on the sole basis of need'. Mark Cutts has produced a devastating critique of the implications of Article 8.[65] He argues that the phrase 'and beyond' was critical in introducing a new dynamic into the process of delivering humanitarian assistance. For the Bosnian Serbs this article extended their control of aid delivered not only to the besieged city of Sarajevo but to all other areas under their control (in particular this encompassed areas such as the eastern safe areas). Furthermore, Cutts argues, the phrase 'non-discriminatory' changed the basis upon which aid was perceived to be delivered from one predicated upon an 'impartial' assessment of needs to one based upon 'reciprocal access' to resources. Instead, the Bosnian Serbs stressed an interpretation of 'non-discriminatory' that emphasised proportionality to 'population'.

Cutts suggests that this led the Bosnian Serbs to perceive an entitlement to some 25 per cent of the total food aid delivered both to and, critically, 'beyond' Sarajevo. This was particularly perverse, in the sense that the Bosnian Serb populations were largely self-sufficient in terms of food production, firewood and winterised accommodation. The perversity of the situation was also accentuated by the agreement serving partially to legitimise and, apparently, to legalise Bosnian Serb obstructionism. This regime applied until late 1995 when the siege was finally lifted by NATO air and Federation ground action.[66]

Given the nature of the concessions and their significance in terms of the wider humanitarian effort, it is perhaps surprising that the agreement, and the airlift resulting from it, continued for so long. This is particularly so given the ease with which aid could increasingly move by land convoy through central Bosnia after the February 1994 Croat–Muslim peace agreements.

Cutts gives two reasons for UNHCR (and more importantly the donor states who led the airlift operation) stubbornly clinging to the idea of maintaining the airlift.[67] First he argues that, once halted, it would have been hard to persuade aircraft-donating countries to resume the operation. The second reason is related to the perceived strategy of some states to substitute humanitarian action for an enforcement strategy. As such, the airlift satisfied the need of several UNHCR donor states to demonstrate that they were making a positive contribution, particularly given the controversies arising from the recognised powerlessness of UNPROFOR. Thus, the airlift increasingly represented a strategy of legitimisation rather than of practical necessity.[68] Arguably, this also debilitated the effectiveness of negotiating strategies for humanitarian access predicated upon and emphasising a 'needs-based' approach.

To some extent, redefining the basis upon which food was distributed was compounded by genuine difficulties among the population in understanding the basis upon which food aid was allocated. In a post-communist society, in which social and economic dependence upon the state was deeply ingrained, the fragmentation of government and the resource shortages created by warfare precipitated a search for alternative sources of assistance.[69] In effect, to many people, the humanitarian programme became conflated to some degree with the role formerly occupied by the communist state. The ability of the humanitarian community to distribute food aid on the basis of 'needs' was, therefore, eroded further by the expectations of a post-communist society. Nevertheless, the demand for food assistance was also precipitated by a search for financial reward.[70] Nor were such motivations limited to the Bosnian Serbs. Cutts, for example, points to the

Bosnian government and Croat authorities selectively stressing population figures rather than 'needs' when it suited them.[71] The result, however, was for UNHCR to adopt a food distribution strategy conducted in a framework of reciprocity but, as Cutts suggests, with 'concessions' sought for areas of outstanding 'need'. In effect this introduced an additional pretext on which aid could be obstructed: namely, inequity.

SYSTEMS AND PROCEDURES NEGOTIATED WITH THE PARTIES[72]

Mechanisms which partially legitimised Serb obstructionism also arose as a consequence of agreements unavoidably or inadvertently negotiated away by UNPROFOR and UNHCR early in the war. For example, in order to ensure their security UNHCR and UNPROFOR both agreed to notify local authorities, in advance, of convoys that would pass through their area, on the understanding that the agencies would be notified when it was not safe for convoys to pass. This system was rapidly exploited as a means for obstructing convoys and evolved to such an extent that all UNHCR convoys effectively required permission to move from the Bosnian Serb Civil Relief Organisation (BSCRO),[73] while UNPROFOR itself required the permission of Bosnian Serb army authorities based at Lukavica barracks to the west of Sarajevo.[74] Both authorities demanded complete and exceptionally detailed passenger and cargo manifests. Even a slight deviation from the details submitted could lead to a refusal to travel or obstruction at checkpoints. These mechanisms could also be used to exert leverage over UNHCR to gain access to more food or to punish the humanitarian community for perceived bias towards other sides. All three belligerent factions acted in this way.

UNHCR's attempts to mitigate accusations of partiality inadvertently compounded the difficulties. A solution appeared to be to make the humanitarian effort more transparent through publishing reports on convoys and deliveries in the form of the monthly plan. Nevertheless, despite the intention of undermining obstructionism through transparency, such reports were frequently seen as providing the belligerents with additional information upon which they could obstruct assistance. In effect, sometimes transparency allowed demands to be quantified more effectively, rather than serving to undermine the basis upon which the demands were constructed. Transparency was also perceived as fuelling demands for more information on convoy movements which, itself, became a mechanism and pretext for obstruction.[75]

'UTILITY POLITICS'

Obstructionism was not limited simply to emergency food relief. Public utilities, such as gas, were vital services if populations were to remain in their homes. Much of Sarajevo's housing and industry was fuelled by gas but the supply lines cut across both Bosnian Serb and Muslim territory.[76] This gave both belligerents the capacity to limit access to essential services as a means of increasing the misery of the besieged population and of extracting advantages from them and the international community.

Obstruction was routine throughout 1992 and 1993, with the Bosnian Serbs frequently cutting the gas supply lines for Sarajevo at Semisvac, while the Muslims responded by cutting the lines which supplied the Serb suburbs. However, as a result of mutual, albeit unequal, dependence, the Bosnian Serbs and Muslims signed an agreement (on 18 November 1993) to the effect that no operations which could jeopardise the distribution of gas elsewhere should be undertaken.[77] While the agreement held for much of 1994, the renewal of fighting at the end of 1994 ensured that utility politics became prevalent again throughout 1995. Such issues were both a symptom and cause of a deteriorating relationship between the warring factions. This was exacerbated by frequent attempts by government forces to precipitate exchanges of fire with the BSA which would endanger civil engineering teams engaged on utility repair projects. Clearly these were part of a wider attempt to draw UNPROFOR itself into the conflict. Publishing the fact that a belligerent was preventing either food or utilities access to its own populations was rarely possible. Positive proof was difficult to find and media access – to publicise it once found – was limited. It would also have compromised UNHCR's ability to remain neutral and impartial, and brought them into direct confrontation with warring factions.

CONCLUSION

The history of negotiations between the humanitarian community and the warring factions in Bosnia–Herzegovina between 1992 and 1995 is replete with problems. However, it is clear that 'linkage' and 'conditionality' were features of the Bosnian condition rather than created by the humanitarian community. More could have been done, both by donors and the humanitarian community itself, to reduce 'linkage'; however, the inescapable fact is that the greatest act of commission was the aggression begun and supported by Milosevic's regime. Nevertheless, the greatest act of omission was the failure of the international community to take an early and robust response to Belgrade's war of aggression. UNPROFOR's consent-based mandate ultimately created UNHCR's dependence upon negotiated access regimes and formal agreements. Of the latter, the Sarajevo airport agreement stands out. The critical situation in Sarajevo in 1992 and then UNHCR's institutional dependence upon its donors and its willingness to reflect their priorities in its own policies ensured the continuation of the agreement even after its practical utility, given the associated costs, had evaporated. This agreement, more than any other, demonstrates the poverty of an international strategy that attempts to use humanitarian assistance as a substitute for an effective engagement with the crisis.

NOTES

1. The views expressed in this article are those of the author and do not necessarily reflect those of the UK Ministry of Defence.
2. See S. Gordon, 'How to Make Safe Areas Unsafe', in S. Gordon and F.H. Toase (eds), *Aspects of Peacekeeping* (Frank Cass: London, 2000), pp. 213–31.
3. *UNHCR Information Notes* (Zagreb: UNHCR, 1994).
4. See M. Cutts, *The Humanitarian Operation in Bosnia, 1992–95: Dilemmas of Negotiating Humanitarian Access*, UNHCR Working Paper No. 8 (Geneva: UNHCR, 1999), p. 2.
5. This was not universal. Gorazde, for example, had an essentially rural economy and consequently its ability to withstand siege by growing its own food ensured that its resilience was much higher than it would otherwise have been.
6. For an excellent discussion of the 'economics' of Bosnia's war see V. Bojicic and M. Kaldor, 'The Political Framing of the War in Bosnia-Herzegovina', in M. Kaldor and B. Vashee, *New Wars: Restructuring the Global Military Sector* (London: Pinter, 1997), pp. 137–77.
7. M. Duffield, *An Account of Relief Operations in Bosnia*, Relief and Rehabilitation Network Paper 3 (London: Overseas Development Institute (ODI), 1994), p. 5. Duffield provides an interesting and comprehensive survey of many of the issues confronting humanitarian agencies in this timely article.
8. Many of the smaller NGOs were entirely dependent on money provided by the multilateral donors. Consequently, they could not generally afford programmes on both sides of the confrontation lines.
9. See J. MacKinlay and R. Kent, 'UN Reform', *World Today*, 53:7 (July 1994).
10. See K. van Brabant in Gordon and Toase (eds), *Aspects of Peacekeeping*.
11. M. Pugh, 'The UNHCR as lead Agency in the Former Yugoslavia', *Journal of Humanitarian Assistance*, http://www-jha.sps.cam.ac.uk/a/a007.htm, posted on 1 April 1996, p. 4. See also, UNHCR, *The State of the World's Refugees: The Challenge of Protection* (London: Penguin, 1995), pp.153 and 177.

12. L. Minear *et al.*, *Humanitarian Action in the Former Yugoslavia: The UN's Role 1991–93*, Occasional Paper No. 18, T.J. Watson, Junior, Institute for International Studies and Refugee Policy Group, 1994.
13. UN General Assembly resolution 2816 (XXVI) of 14 December 1971.
14. Pugh describes the shortcomings of the coordination mechanisms before the Gulf War as well as the UN Disaster Relief Organisations lack of capacity for contingency planning and emergency preparedness during the Kurdish exodus from Iraq in 1991. He also highlights UNDP's experience as a developmental agency providing it with insufficient experience of emergencies to operate effectively as a coordination structure in a complex emergency. See Pugh, 'The UNHCR as lead Agency', p. 2.
15. Pugh, 'The UNHCR as lead Agency', p. 3.
16. Ibid.
17. Despite the apparently high numbers, between January and December 1996 IFOR Civil Affairs Officers dealt with over 300 NGO's operating in Bosnia. Interview with Major A. Mack, G5 Coordinator for Multinational Division South-West, Nato's IFOR.
18. Where they are predominantly from one side it reduces the room for impartiality or neutrality.
19. Pugh, 'The UNHCR as lead Agency', p. 9.
20. Background interviews with UNICEF staff.
21. Pugh, 'The UNHCR as lead Agency', p. 9.
22. Interview with Lieutenant-Colonel Renolleau, Eagleton Office (Sarajevo), L. Vissert (UNHCR) and J. Carter (UN Civil Affairs).
23. Interview with Lanwe Vissert, UNHCR.
24. The principles used to characterise the relationship between the UNHCR and the NGOs are drawn from Mark Duffield's excellent study, *An Account of Relief Operations in Bosnia*, Relief and Rehabilitation Network Paper 3 (London: ODI, 1994).
25. Ibid.
26. Cutts, *The Humanitarian Operation in Bosnia*, p. 2.
27. Furthermore, the belligerents and UNPROFOR preferred to deal with one lead agency rather than with hundreds of NGOs. Such a mechanism was also expected to enable UNPROFOR more easily to determine which organisations they were mandated to support.
28. Cutts, *The Humanitarian Operation in Bosnia*, p. 2.
29. Ibid., p. 9.
30. For a fuller treatment of this see S. Gordon, 'How to Make Safe areas Unsafe', in Gordon and Toase, *Aspects of Peacekeeping*.
31. Interview with Sergio V. de Mello, UN Emergency Relief Coordinator.
32. Interviews with Colonel R. Stewart, Brigadier A. Duncan and Colonel P. Williams. See also P.G. Williams, 'Tactical Command in Bosnia, Operation GRAPPLE 3 November 1993–May 1994', paper presented to the Camberley Army Staff College, 22 September 1994.
33. Duffield, *An Account of Relief Operations in Bosnia*, p. 5.
34. Ibid.
35. ECHO, 'European Community Humanitarian Office Humanitarian Aid Annual Report – 1994' (Brussels: ECHO/EU Office of Information, 1994). Also quoted in Duffield, *An Account of Relief Operations in Bosnia*, p. 5.
36. J. Macrae and N. Leader, *Shifting Sands: The Search for 'Coherence' between*

Political and Humanitarian Responses to Complex Political Emergencies, HPG Report No. 8 (London: Overseas Development Institute, 2000). See also M. Aaronson, 'NGOs and the Military in Complex Emergencies', unpublished mimeo, 2001, and background interviews with Department for International Development staff.

37. Duffield, *An Account of Relief Operations in Bosnia*, p. 5.
38. Interviews with Squadron Leader K. Harding and Flight Lieutenant J. Kendall, former UN military observers.
39. These were usually the single-delivery NGOs (groups of people who collected what they viewed as emergency relief aid and delivered it personally).
40. UNPROFOR was mandated to provide escorts only to UNHCR-accredited NGOs. Furthermore, UNPROFOR liaison officers and UNHCR field officer networks provided the most capable organisation for negotiating access to central Bosnian towns – hence accentuating reliance and confirming the perceived (by warring factions) conflation of the two organisations.
41. UNHCR, *Working with the Military* (Geneva: UNHCR, 1995), p. 50.
42. Duffield, *An Account of Relief Operations in Bosnia*, p. 5.
43. See J. de Courten (ICRC Director of Operations), 'Humanitarian Action and Peacekeeping Operations', paper presented to ICRC's 1994 conference, p. 29.
44. Cutts, *The Humanitarian Operation in Bosnia*, p. 2.
45. Interview with senior UNPROFOR officers in Sarajevo, 1995.
46. Cutts, *The Humanitarian Operation in Bosnia*, p. 2.
47. Interview with senior UNPROFOR officers in Sarajevo, 1995.
48. Ibid.
49. However, UNHCR was forced by the Secretary-General, himself under pressure from permanent members of the Security Council, to restart their operations.
50. Interviews with Lanwe Vissert (UNHCR) and Brigadier John Reith (former Commander HQ Sector South-West).
51. Interview with Lieutenant-Colonel D. Santa Olalla, former Gorazde force commander.
52. This point is drawn from an interview with Lieutenant-Colonel B. Watters of the Cheshire regiment but is also made by Mark Duffield in *Duffield, An Account of Relief Operations in Bosnia*, p. 5.
53. Cutts, *The Humanitarian Operation in Bosnia*, p. 2.
54. Karadzic finally agreed to Madame Ogata's request to this on 18 November 1993; however, the BSA failed to implement it. Contained in 'Note by UNHCR on the Implementation of the Commitments Made by the Bosnian Leaders on 18 November 1993 and Subsequently' (Geneva: UNHCR, 20 December 1993), p. 4.
55. The HVO (Bosnian Croat Army) and the BSA (Bosnian Serb Army) in particular.
56. The ODA document 'Convoy Operations Following the 18 and 29 November Agreements' (London: ODA, 17 December 1993), p. 1, details that only 52 per cent of the biweekly requirement of 21,000 metric tonnes carried by road and air was actually delivered in the month following the November agreements. It attributes obstructions to a list of bureaucratic, administrative and security requirements ranging from unusual visa arrangements for UNHCR drivers through to the direct taxation of UNHCR

fuel purchases (a 30 per cent charge was levied by the Croatian government from December 1993), low-level harassment, the shooting of an UNPROFOR IL-76 aircraft landing at Sarajevo airport on 20 December 1993 (six shots through the wing) and the shelling of ICRC staff engaged in the actual process of exchanging prisoners of war and refugees.

57. General Lewis Mackenzie, Chief of Staff of UNPROFOR, and Cedric Thornberry, Head of Civil Affairs. The agreement's status in international law results from Security Council Resolution 761 (29 June 1992) which required full compliance from all of the parties.

58. For a full discussion of the UNPROFOR mandate see W. Durch and J. Schear, 'Faultlines: UN Operations in the Former Yugoslavia', in W. Durch (ed.), *Peacekeeping, American Policy and the Uncivil Wars of the 1990s* (Basingstoke: Macmillan, 1997), pp. 193–275.

59. Altogether some 160,000 tonnes of food, medicines and other goods were delivered to Sarajevo in over 12,000 flights. In addition to aid delivery, the airlift was used for the medical evacuation of more than 1,100 casualties. Kris Janowski, UNHCR Press Briefing, 18 April 1995, Sarajevo.

60. Interview with Lou Townsend, UNHCR liaison officer to UNPROFOR's BHC HQ. The worst incident was the shooting down of an Italian air force aircraft on 3 September 1992 by a surface-to-air missile.

61. *Report of the Secretary-General Pursuant to General Assembly Resolution 53/35 (1998) 'Srebrenica Report'*, Advance Copy for Delegations, 15 November 1995, p. 11.

62. For a discussion of the possibilities for humanitarian war in Bosnia from 1992 see R. Lyman, 'Possibilities for Humanitarian War by the International Community in Bosnia-Herzegovina 1992–1995', *Journal of Humanitarian Assistance, http://www.jha.sps.cam.ac.uk/a/a001.htm*, posted 15 July 1997.

63. Article 6 of the agreement.

64. Interview with Lou Townsend, UNHCR.

65. Cutts, *The Humanitarian Operation in Bosnia*, p. 2.

66. For a detailed examination of how the war was brought to an end see T. Ripley, *Operation Deliberate Force: The UN and NATO Campaign in Bosnia 1995* (Lancaster: Centre for Defence and International Security Studies, 1999).

67. Cutts, *The Humanitarian Operation in Bosnia*, p. 2.

68. For an excellent discussion of how donors manipulated UNHCR's response to the humanitarian crisis in Bosnia in a way that reflected their requirements rather than the needs of Bosnia's displaced population, see Pugh, 'The UNHCR as lead Agency'.

69. Background interviews with UNHCR staff.

70. For example, in late 1994 the Bosnian Serbs cut off virtually all of the gas and electricity supplies to Sarajevo and obstructed all deliveries of firewood and coal, promising to restore normality in exchange for increasing Serb access to firewood to 50 per cent. However, because the Serbs enjoyed almost unhindered access to wood and comprised less than 25 per cent of the population, UNHCR refused to compromise for nearly eight months. Only when the humanitarian situation became pressing did UNHCR concede that the Serbs could have access to 38 per cent of supplies.

71. For example, pressure from Croat authorities in Herceg-Bosna, which controlled the two main road routes into central Bosnia, led to significant

diversions of UNHCR food to Croat areas.

72. Cutts, *The Humanitarian Operation in Bosnia*, p. 9.
73. Interview with Lanwe Vissert, UNHCR.
74. Interview with Captain Guy Lavender, ADC to General Rupert Smith, Commander UNPROFOR.
75. Duffield, *An Account of Relief Operations in Bosnia*, p. 5.
76. Interview with former UNPROFOR chief engineer, David Craig.
77. See *UNHCR Information Notes on the Former Yugoslavia*, No. 12/93 (Zagreb: UNHCR, December 1993), p. 3.

5

Inequity in Outcome: Who Really 'Wins' in a Military Negotiation?

DEBORAH GOODWIN

Peacekeeping is not a soldier's job, but only a soldier can do it.[1]

INTRODUCTION

What I hope to do in this chapter is to place a question in your mind: is the idea of a 'win/win' outcome realistic in an operational environment? Can there ever be equity in resolution in a military negotiating scenario, or is this just a neat catchphrase which might apply to commercial negotiation situations alone? More importantly, does a soldier aspire to an even win/win solution in a real world and tactical level negotiating scenario? Might it not be more desirable to achieve a resolution in one's own favour?

It may be more appropriate to describe any military attempt at negotiating at the tactical level of operations as being *coercive diplomacy* rather than pure negotiation since there are several delineating factors present when a soldier encounters a negotiating situation which might be underestimated in terms of constriction of thought and the scope for decision-making. Armed forces are often expected to act as instruments for political policy-makers, and are intrinsically linked with governing political elites in a social and practical sense. That is not to say that a soldier implicitly holds the same ideologies as the political masters, but with the blurring of specific military with non-military roles and expectations, inevitable tensions arise for the serving soldier concerning methodologies and ideologies versus rules of engagement (ROE) and standard operating procedures (SOPs). Van Doorn points out some of these tensions:

There is also a differentiation in orientation between the combat-commander complex and the technical-managerial complex. It is an open question whether it is possible to integrate both types of orientation, which also include a difference in ideological outlook. At this moment the traditional uniform concept of the soldier has become diffuse and ambiguous.[2]

Returning to the description of military micro-negotiation as *coercive diplomacy*, Alexander George in his book on this subject pinpoints such an allusion stemming from the John F. Kennedy development and recognition of a pertinent use of such a tactic in a military context in the 1960s:[3]

> ... the employment of force is coupled with – i.e. preceded, accompanied, or followed by – appropriate communications to the opponent. The coercive strategy therefore, has a signalling, bargaining, negotiating character that is built into the conceptualisation and conduct of military operations, a feature absent in the traditional military strategy.[4]

This would appear to be a valid description of military micro-negotiation *per se*, defining the more specialised nature of the scenarios, and of the governing factors for the soldier in any such process. It allows for the military 'steps of procedure' for response (as probably outlined in the specific ROEs and blue cards distributed before deployment). The soldier may not be choosing to use armed response in the first instance to deal with a problem, but the potential to do so remains, should it be deemed necessary. Similarly the strictures on what a soldier might be able to 'give' in any bargaining situation can be recognised: very often a soldier has little or nothing materially with which to bargain, and in the final instance coercion or armed force may be the main, or indeed only, bargaining chip.

> A little while back there was a Finn soldier who was shot at from a Greek village. The Finns drove up their armoured cars and threatened to shoot the whole village right there and then if there was another shooting. This was the only correct thing to do. Otherwise the Cyps think you're free game. You have to protect your men above all else. But the Fincon commander was in serious trouble after that. The Headquarters civilians really took after him. 'No, no, no. You can't touch a hair on a Cypriot.' But I'd do the same thing.[5]

A comment such as the above reinforces the common frustration amongst the military between knowing when to take a combative and non-combative stance in a peacekeeping situation, and when to shift between the two. Often the ROEs can be non-specific in giving guidance as to at what point this shift is to be made, being as it is so dependent on external and subjective factors. A soldier will have a prime concern for safety of personnel in the vast majority of incidents, and this is likely to be a governing factor in a soldier's decision-making in such situations. Rightly so, when personnel have been deployed into an operational area as peacekeepers and have a duty to carry out specific tasks and requirements. But when military micro-negotiation is employed, there may be other factors at play which govern assessment and reassessment of the situation and the tactical response to it: factors which may be mirrored in higher-level political negotiation situations, but not business negotiation encounters.

PROBLEMS OF COERCIVE DIPLOMACY

We may ask if the concept of *coercive diplomacy* brings inherent problems of its own. Alexander George[6] outlines six main concerns which arise when coercive diplomacy is employed, and it is worth taking a moment to assess these in the context of military negotiation.

1. Risks of ultimatum. (Will the ultimatum be provocative?)

An ultimatum is likely in military micro-negotiation if prevailing factors do not allow for a lengthy or detailed bargaining process. If the soldier has nothing to 'bargain' with, i.e. if the orders dictate one line of action only with no deviation, the likely response to any opposition against the achievement of this objective will be forceful, perhaps even provocative: 'This convoy is coming through this roadblock, and if you don't move out of the way, I'll make you move.' The degree of provocation such an ultimatum might exert on the opponent depends on the latter's own 'military' security and assurance in terms of back-up support, or the prior agreement from their policy-makers on the scale of aggressive action to be taken within a conflict zone. Therefore responses could range from submission to a firefight. The military micro-negotiator will need to be aware of this range of response to an ultimatum, and realise that speedy reassessment and response will be needed following such a statement. In bargaining terms it is not possible to back down from an ultimatum, as it is the ultimate threat. The next move, on either side, is likely to be force.

2. *Conflict between crisis-management and coercive diplomacy. (Will adherence to requirements of crisis-management dilute sense of urgency needed for coercion?)*

The soldier is prone to experiencing a conflict between crisis-management and coercion when 'on the ground' in a bargaining scenario. A soldier's 'crisis-management' is the provision of specific ROEs, which may change as the context of the operation changes in an attempt to keep pace with shifts in political/social manœuvres in the geographical area. This factor represents the vague area which can arise between applying force and continuing discussion: at what precise point in a confrontation must the decision to shift response be made; which rules of behaviour and method-ology should be followed at which stage (a dilemma which reflects George's factor of the timing of negotiation)?

Such a threat can only work in deterrent terms if the opponent is convinced of the likelihood of implementation. For the soldier this can be both useful and self-destructive. Supposing, for instance, the opponent knows the ROEs and how to manipulate the soldier's responses. (Knowledge of the ROEs can allow an opponent to operate a policy of brinkmanship against a soldier, thus frustrating the military bargainer.) Comments such as those cited below stem from this kind of scenario:

> We're sent here with our hands tied behind our backs. We're like traffic cops, we can only wave our hands. The politicians won't let us have any authority. If we could use a little muscle, this whole mess would be over in two weeks.[7]

> Bullshitting, bullshitting all the time.[7]

3. *Timing of strong coercive threats. (Has opponent been sufficiently impressed with your determination to see the threat as credible?)*

Often in military negotiation a crucial factor is *time*. If a soldier has ample time in which to manœuvre and build the process of negotiations, then there is unlikely to be a conflict of governing guidelines and principles, or at least more of a breathing space in which to alter decisions and approaches if necessary. But frequently a soldier can be faced with a sudden block to the successful implementation of orders, and the remedial process can move and escalate extremely quickly. Lack of time can lead to ill-considered responses and poorly judged moves being made. It can work two ways of course: not allowing one's opponent sufficient time to think can disorientate and confuse them. An UNPROFOR officer describes his use of this tactic: 'I decided to give him no time to think. We jumped back into the Warrior and headed straight for the roadblock. They were so surprised that no response was made at all. I achieved my objectives.'

Too much time in a micro-negotiation can be destructive as it can weaken the urgency for movement and progression towards an outcome. So allowing an opponent too long to consider options can be equally destructive to one's own cause.

The timing of threats follows on from this appreciation of the *time* factor itself, as the following incident shows:

> In 1967 the Dancon commander went down to an OP [observation post] on the Green Line where a Danish soldier had been disarmed by some Turkish fighters. He went down there with an automatic weapon and waved it at the Turks. He threatened to shoot the whole bunch right there on the spot. It worked. But it got the commander into a lot of trouble with the civilians back at Headquarters. They were out of their minds.[8]

4. *Timing of negotiations. (Can negotiations be viable until opponent is sufficiently impressed with your determination?)*

In other words, it may be the case that the duration of the negotiation could be an important factor in the decision-making process and influence the response from the other party. If a negotiator is prepared to persevere, it might indicate to the other party that there is a wish to achieve a mutually acceptable negotiated outcome, whatever the circumstances.

5. *Content of carrot and stick. (Are the carrot and stick adequate to overcome opponent's disinclination to accept demand?)*

A dangerous situation can arise if the other party views the threat as merely a bluff; the deliverer of the threat is then forced to carry out at least part of the threat to re-establish a situational powerbase. This could have serious military implications, escalating to strategic and political implications.[9] The 'carrot and stick' available to the soldier may be limited to an option of the other party conceding before or after the use of force. Frequently there are few other 'carrots' which can be used to appeal to an opponent.[10] The nature of the 'stick' is more obvious.

6. *Timing of carrot and stick. (Can the carrot and stick be applied before military actions harden the opponent's determination?)*

It may be the case that an implied use of force, or a threat, could pre-empt an escalatory response in another party (although there remains a risk that an opposite reaction might occur). Negotiation remains at once one of the most important but least practised of the skills required in peacekeeping.

In order to examine these hypotheses further, let us review an example of an early operational scenario where tactical level negotiation came to the fore. The UN Protection Force in Bosnia-Herzegovina (UNPROFOR) witnessed the unique experience of the dichotomy between peacemaking and peacekeeping. Though the UN had a limited humanitarian mandate in Bosnia-Herzegovina in mid 1992, it had neither the resources nor mandate to embark on large-scale peacemaking, which, in some respects, did not get underway until September 1992. This made the position of UNPROFOR on the ground virtually untenable at times. Negotiating solutions to political problems, and implementing such solutions, is a logical division of functions. But solutions cannot be found without reference to realities on the ground and the process of implementation of agreed solutions is not a mechanical one as it requires an ongoing process, *in situ*, of consultation and negotiation with the relevant parties.

For example, it was some three months after initial deployment that UN professional 'negotiators' joined the HQ.[11] A British soldier described the difficulties of the situation: 'Arriving in Bosnia and attempting to grasp the complexities of the situation has been likened to trying to take a sip of water from a fire hydrant. Our preparation package went some way to controlling this gush, or at least to warning us that we were about to be soaked.'

Civil Affairs (CA) personnel were used by the deployed Canadian troops to supplement information and intelligence for troops on the ground, and to conduct as many negotiations as possible (obviously prearranged as opposed to *ad hoc*).[12] It was felt that by involving the CA group early on and in negotiations over disputes between locals and the military, it freed the troop commander from an additional time-consuming burden. Since none of the team spoke Serbo-Croat or Macedonian, local contract translators were hired and used for local–military liaison. It was stated that the use of these local translators in conjunction with CA members proved successful in many aspects of the peacekeeping mission. Many lessons were learned from this experience, especially that whenever possible a CA group should be used to coordinate/negotiate civil–military operations, since the UN does not as yet have a specific unit charged with CA team-type duties. Using the attached team to coordinate civil–military projects which help to win hearts and minds proved useful, as did the fact that the team could provide intelligence and assessment on what was happening on the ground. Of more immediate importance was the growing recognition that the more soldiers knew about the global picture and how the mandate was to be applied on the ground, the easier it was for them to react properly to situations and to conduct effective low-level negotiations. As one corporal observed:

> You have to learn to do it on the spot. Technically we shouldn't have to negotiate, if we catch someone in the zone, we're a section of men, they've got a weapon, you know, we could do the military thing, put his face to the ground, take it away, and haul him out. But we don't do that. We negotiate for the weapons, because that's the way it's come down through orders.[13]

NEGOTIATING SKILLS

Given the coercive nature of tactical military negotiation, we may ask if the average soldier is equipped with the necessary negotiating skills. Would it not be more realistic to assume that the attributes fostered by army training tend to run counter to those needed in the bargaining process, and that supplementary training might be needed?

Figure 5.1 suggests the broadly defined attributes which a soldier appears to possess as part of his operational role, and compares them with recognised negotiating skills. By suggesting main attributes in both domains, it is possible to speculate that there are several possible areas of weakness, or at least limitation, when a soldier negotiates. This is understandable when one acknowledges the multiplicity of tasks which the modern soldier is expected to perform.

In the civilian world a professional negotiator is usually trained thoroughly and works in a basically rational environment, without fear for his/her life (unless taking part in police operation or hostage-negotiation, for example). He or she applies procedures and protocols which have been gleaned from theoretical and observable contexts, and will become practised and conversant with a diversity of negotiating styles and techniques. It is a complex skill which is honed and modified repeatedly, with as little personal cost to the negotiator as possible.

Compare this with the context within which low-level military negotiations take place. Soldiers are professional combatants, not professional negotiators, who are placed in a chaotic and dangerous working environment. Within this environment they must ply their trade, diverse as it is, with only a brief pre-operational negotiating training, if they are lucky. Micro-negotiation will not be a familiar procedure; the counterparts are diverse in nature, often physically threatening and irrational through the

FIGURE 5.1. Comparison of key negotiating skills with normal military attributes.[14]

Key negotiating attributes	*Akin to* broadly defined *soldier attributes?*	
	YES	NO
planning and preparation	✓	
knowledge of subject under negotiation	✓	
ability to think clearly under pressure	✓	
ability to communicate clearly	✓	
listening skills (prolonged)		✗
integrity	✓	
persuasion	✓	
ability to win the confidence of others	✓	
problem-solving skills	✓	
self-control	✓	
persistence	✓	
insight	✓	
ability to exploit available power	✓	
leadership and control	✓	
previous negotiating experience		✗
tolerance of other viewpoints		✗
competitiveness	✓	
debating ability	✓	
willingness to be disliked	✓	
tolerance of ambiguity		✗
appropriate body language		✗
trust	✓	
willingness to take personal career risk		✗
use of force	✓	
work with an interpreter		✗
appreciation of time		✗

influence of either alcohol, drugs and adrenaline – or a mixture of all three.[15] The implications of getting it wrong could be horrendous – for the soldier, his colleagues, the counterparts, or the operational scenario and context. The soldier is required to employ material and concepts which have not formed part of basic training, and, even at a junior level, he will be required to work to a higher level of competence than is normally expected. The reason for this is the possibility that the decisions made by the soldier on the ground, good or bad, can have effects above and beyond the tactical level. A key is for the soldier to have the self-confidence to carry out such work effectively and assuredly. Temperament is also important. As a Finnish peacekeeper observed: 'It is a good thing the Finnish character is suitable for peacekeeping. We can take many insults. It takes a lot to arouse us. Nothing gets us excited … 95 per cent of this job is not getting excited … Only soldiers with this temperament can be peacekeepers.'

Most junior military personnel have had little experience of real micro-negotiation prior to a deployment, and therefore the learning curve is a steep one.[16] A great deal of knowledge comes from informal conversations with colleagues and 'learning on the job', which must be a hit and miss affair to say the least. As a Canadian corporal put it: 'You have to learn it on the spot.'

BARGAINING

Another common characteristic of negotiation is the realisation that the bargainers do not ask for what they really want, and this forms part of the movement towards the common ground. Usually demands are greater in scope than a party can expect to obtain. Therefore it is extremely difficult for one party to gauge the precise nature of what the other wants from the process, or even if they want to bargain. Most negotiations start with an element of competitiveness rather than cooperation, which can promote mutual suspicion and mistrust. A soldier is trained to be unambiguous in the delivery of information and in the analysis of received information, since within military operations a lack of clarity can be costly in both time and logistical terms. Ambiguity is not tolerated or expected. Thus it may be reasonable to expect that a soldier might find this aspect of the negotiating process to be frustrating, if not annoying.

Ambiguity might reveal itself in indirect communication as well, which may be hard to read and interpret. Often glances, tentative statements, or the failure to mention a specific demand, are signs indicative of a communication which can be explored. The problem is that a signal must be noticeable, and often clues are missed, even by an expert negotiator. Since signals employ the connotative meanings of words they are not precise or clear in meaning, and this is something a soldier is taught to avoid and may be likely to miss, or even dismiss, in a negotiation.

TIME

Ambiguity and a gradual development towards negotiated agreement can take time and be laborious. As the pressure of time increases, so the desire to reach an agreement is enhanced. Perceptions of 'wasted time' might increase also if a party is intolerant of periods of perceived inactivity. A fundamental aspect of a soldier's training is the desire to achieve a resolution as quickly and efficiently as possible. This is a prime requirement in tactical terms. In a military operation the time factor can be critical, if not pivotal. The following comments and observations from peace-keeping soldiers indicate that this is one of the most frustrating elements in military negotiation:

> Held there for two hours …

> … very long and tedious journey … many roadblocks …

> … the convoy had been trapped for two hours …

> … negotiation at all levels is essential … this may take time …

> … if possible let your counterpart start, and hear him out, don't interrupt, be patient …

> … discussion/negotiations with town elders can be an interesting and sometimes frustrating experience. Be patient, because they will take a long time to gather and meet with you …

Bearing in mind that soldiers have an inbuilt drive to resolve situations as quickly as possible, pre-negotiation stages may be neglected or skimped, thus making for a more difficult negotiation process in the long run.

Tolerance of the time issue, other viewpoints and no obvious movement towards a resolution can be difficult for a soldier to deal with, given the proactive nature of the profession. Negotiation is difficult if the professional inclination is to achieve the aim speedily and efficiently, and even more difficult if the people involved are acting in circumstances which are beyond their control and definitely not run of the mill. Additional political and military pressures further complicate any tactical micro-negotiation.

Where the military micro-negotiator has an obvious advantage over a professional civilian negotiator is over the matter of force, or 'turning up the heat' in a negotiation, as one officer put it. The force which can be used is obvious and visual, but the fine line comes at the point at which force becomes aggressive intent or is used when unprovoked.

Sometimes a low-key response is appropriate, as this scenario, described by a Canadian peacekeeper, illustrates: 'One incident I was involved with ended up with the Serbian Army showing up with rocket launchers threatening to blow us up. We basically said "Go **** yourselves". They backed down.' On this occasion the above comment worked as a de-escalation tactic; on another it might have had the opposite effect. But it does appear that on many occasions the deflation of any 'military' posturing can have the desired de-escalation effect, perhaps because it is linked with a diminution of the counterpart's standing as a professional soldier. Many serving soldiers have told the author that they have used such retorts to move away from conflict in a micro-negotiation, using the 'You've got them, we've got them' riposte. Lieutenant C., a subaltern on Operation Grapple, resorted to a little friendly instruction to defuse a situation:

> I tried to persuade them that the RPG and rocket launchers would have no effect on my Warrior. They were not convinced, so I pointed out the fact that if they wanted to fire it they should firstly extend it and secondly point it the right way round! The commander of the checkpoint felt embarrassed and this seemed to do the trick.

NEGATIVE EQUITY

In a military negotiation context it is unrealistic to expect that both sides will emerge from a negotiation equally successfully. When armed force can be the ultimate bargaining factor it brings with it expectations and demands which are rarely seen in non-military negotiation. One side has to back down, has to be seen to submit to a greater force or pressure from the other party. The potential use of arms by either negotiator creates a bargaining context which cannot allow for equity in resolution. The stakes are too high, as they would be, for example, in a police negotiation.

Experience in operational areas such as Cyprus show that appropriate techniques exist at the tactical level where peacekeepers have used arbitration, go-between mediation and conciliation to achieve their ends. Principled negotiation, consultation and problem-solving set-ups are more progressive forms of conflict-resolution, if the aim is to do more than just keep the belligerents apart physically.

> Given that the peacekeeping model is changing, it is fair to ask if the tasks that soldiers are now being required to do are still covered in training or general war, or if the changing face of peacekeeping now raises the imperative to train soldiers at all levels in skills that are beyond those needed to successfully prosecute combat operations. Based on experiences from the unstable environment during the Cyprus War in 1974, media reports from events in the former Yugoslavia, Cambodia, and Somalia and an informal survey conducted with several hundred troops who served in Sarajevo with the Canadian Contingent in UNPROFOR, the answer is tentatively 'yes'.[17]

Many soldiers have stated that their experiences in Bosnia, for example, indicated to them that one was either a good negotiator or not, and a person had little time to alter that fact. They were conscious that poorly handled negotiations could have serious ramifications beyond the immediate issue, and when cultural factors and pervading hostility were added then issues and tempers escalated in intensity. A great deal of damage could be done with very few words, and this realisation was daunting.

At the heart of this chapter is the hypothesis that if a soldier succeeds in a micro-negotiation setting it will be because he has 'defeated' the other party in some way, either through words or with the threat of armed response. Negotiation has been used to achieve this end, but coercion may have dictated the final resolution. In non-hostile tactical negotiations there may be scope for a mutually beneficial outcome and more room to work towards a 'win/win' resolution. However, if the soldier is facing a more aggressive counterpart in a more volatile operating environment, then it is likely that there will be a more obvious winner from an encounter, since the factors of mission, time and force play their part in a military negotiation and its outcome. Undoubtedly, soldiers can be extremely effective negotiators, but their operating context is significantly different from that of any commercial negotiator, and therefore optimal resolution outcomes are likely to be different also.

CONCLUSION

In the above example of a roadblock negotiation, the soldier will either 'win' and go through, or 'lose' and turn around (i.e. he goes through or he does not go through). Rarely can there be equity in resolution in such a situation. Thus it may be useful when one considers the soldier as a negotiator to recognise that he (or she) is in an entirely different bargaining context from those depicted in business and commercial negotiation manuals. It is unrealistic to expect that a soldier can carry out neat, equitable bargaining scenarios in an operational context which will be making numerous and often conflicting demands on that soldier. There are many other factors at play, none of which are replicated in a safe, structured business negotiation, and there tend to be more obvious winners and losers from a negotiating encounter within a military operational area.

If this is the case then the next question to be asked is: how should the soldier be trained to negotiate within this hostile working scenario, given some of the frustrations voiced? It may be that a soldier will need more context-specific training in this skill, and some of this specific training could run contrary to many of the established negotiation 'do's and don'ts' outlined in existing commercial training manuals on the subject. Perhaps the negotiation training book for the serving soldier should be rewritten, at least in part. It may be pertinent for serving personnel to be aware that while they *negotiate* whenever they can, in fact they *coerce* every time they encounter such a situation. Whatever the case, the implications and pressures being placed on the modern soldier in the world of observable peacekeeping are considerable. Perhaps the last word should go to an anonymous Canadian soldier: 'You need an army of trained men who are not used to shooting at everything ... Peacekeeping brings out the qualities of the best soldier. We just have to change our outmoded ideas as to what makes a soldier.'

NOTES

1. Non-attributable unofficial 'motto' of the UN soldier.
2. M. Janowitz and J. van Doorn, *On Military Ideology* (Rotterdam: Rotterdam University Press, 1971), p. xxvi.
3. 'Let us begin anew, remembering on both sides that civility is not a sign of weakness, that sincerity is always subject to proof. Let us never negotiate out of fear, but let us never fear to negotiate', John F. Kennedy, cited in G.I. Nierenberg, *The Art of Negotiating* (Crandury, NJ: Barnes & Noble, 1968).
4. Alexander George, in George, Hall and Simons, *The Limits of Coercive Diplomacy* (Boston, MA: Little, Brown, 1971), p. 18.
5. Irish officer, UNICYP, cited in Janowitz and van Doorn, *On Military Ideology*, p. 257.
6. In George, Hall and Simons, *The Limits of Coercive Diplomacy*, p. 232.
7. Canadian officer, UNICYP, cited in Janowitz and van Doorn, *On Military Ideology*, p. 252.
8. Danish Officer, UNICYP, ibid., p. 257.
9. T. Schelling, *Arms and Influence* (New York: Colonial Press, 1966), reinforces this aspect of using compliance as a block to a spiralling effect of escalated conflict: 'A deterrent threat usually enjoys some connectedness between the proscribed action and the threatened response' (p. 86), and 'military potential is used to influence other countries, their government or their people ... There is no name for this kind of diplomacy' (p. vi).
10. Except perhaps the use of personal rations, chocolate or small personal belongings which can be quite influential in certain cultures, especially Africa.
11. Information from non-attributable international military sources (unclassified).
12. Reference report, EX Venom Strike, December 1995, filename: CALL0011.
13. Corporal, Interview 2, in J.D.D. Smith, *Canada in Croatia: Peacekeeping and UN Reform – the View from the Ground* (London: HMSO, 1995), p. 32.
14. Adapted from Major Todd Harmanson, 'Negotiating at the Lower Tactical

Level in Peace Operations', MA thesis, Fort Leavenworth, Kansas, 1996.
15. 'The individual may be too intoxicated, angry or mentally deficient to carry on a logical discussion' (non-attributable comment).
16. As from 1995 officer cadets at the Royal Military Academy Sandhurst receive negotiation training as part of their commissioning course. The subject was devised and introduced by the author into Communication Studies training, with effect from 1995 onwards.
17. Dr Kenneth Eyre, comment at symposium on 'The Changing Face of Peace-keeping', Canadian Institute of Strategic Studies, 1993.

6

Civil Affairs Leads the Military into the Twenty-First Century

ASHLEY STOCKER

Of all the many and varied facets of SHAEF's great task, the most vexatious and the least satisfactory was undoubtedly all that complex activity known collectively as Civil Affairs (Lieutenant-General Sir Frederick Morgan, 1950).

When the Cold War juddered to a halt in 1989, military planning staff in many countries of the world found that a new type of mission rapidly filled the void. The sheltered and simple life of planning for a war of survival, against a well-defined and understood threat has been replaced by a series of relatively small-scale and brutal wars where people are struggling to define who they are. It is likely that, during the next decade, the armed forces of NATO and the Partners for Peace will continue to be used in this new role as 'intervention forces' (Spybey, 1996). It is due to such operations that Civil Affairs is enjoying a quiet but firm renaissance in the early twenty-first century. This article sets out to explain the background to the renewed need for Civil Affairs in military operations and describes some of the key skills required for success.

There are strong arguments to retain the ability of military forces to undertake traditional war-fighting operations, such as the Gulf War in 1990/91, in order to maintain a credible defence capability. However, current warfare now tends to be perceived as fitting somewhere into an operational continuum, as seen in Figure 6.1. For the foreseeable future NATO is unlikely to have the comfort of a specific threat on which to focus. NATO or its member states are increasingly going to be asked to provide forces to work in a state of transition where the protection of civilians, not the defeating of an enemy, is central to the mission.

FIGURE 6.1. The operational continuum.[1]

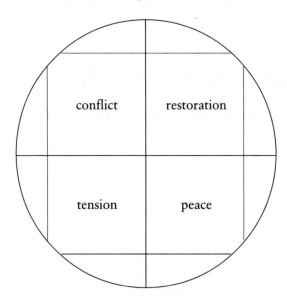

In the past, a mission was considered to be complete when peace broke out and the impact of civil and political dimensions were limited, as shown in Figure 6.2a. The shift of emphasis away from military to political and civilian considerations since the end of the Cold War is demonstrated in Figure 6.2b. This shift in mission focus requires military commanders and staff to understand political and civil factors that could largely be ignored when planning operations during the Cold War era. It is no longer possible for commanders to concentrate solely on the military considerations of an operational deployment, as achievement of the military end-state is unlikely to signal the end of the overarching mission. As a consequence, military commanders are now also expected to understand the civilian and political end-states and may be called upon to help facilitate their implementation.

The requirement for the military to understand the civil and political dimensions of a mission is why Civil Affairs has been removed from the attic of history and is gradually being reinstated as an accepted capability. In the current climate of increasingly slender defence budgets and multiple deployments, missions need to be achieved with the minimum resources possible. If used correctly, Civil Affairs can act as a capability multiplier by reducing the need for force protection and projection. This is achieved through timely and accurate advice to military commanders of appropriate approaches to take towards the civilian population. The facilitation of the military mission can be enhanced, if Civil Affairs

FIGURE 6.2a. The Cold War political–military mission interface.[2]

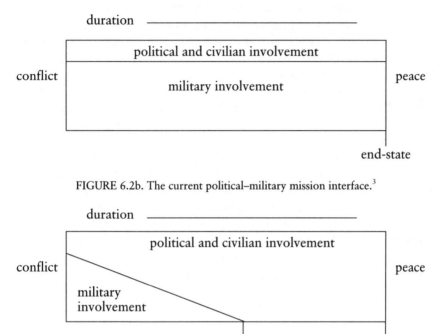

FIGURE 6.2b. The current political–military mission interface.[3]

operators are given the freedom to communicate effectively with the civilian actors in an area of operations.

As with any topic it is probably wise to define what exactly is meant by the term being discussed. The following provides a working definition of Civil Affairs:[3] 'Civil Affairs are the activities in support of military operations embracing the interaction between the military force and humanitarian relief organisations, civilian authorities and the populace, which foster the development of favourable attitudes, emotions and behaviours in neutral, friendly, or hostile groups.'

While many military commanders accept and increasingly demand some form of Civil Affairs capability during operational commitments, frequently little is done to integrate this capability into the force structure prior to deployment. In order fully to understand current and projected missions, all troops deploying to an operational theatre should have an understanding of Civil Affairs and the political and civilian environment in which they will be expected to function. Civil Affairs should be a part of all commanders' planning and preparation for missions and should not be omitted or left to the last minute, as there will inevitably be a price to be paid if these factors are neglected.

If mission planning is to be comprehensive, Civil Affairs ought to be considered alongside other traditional military factors. In the ideal mission the military role might simply be to provide a stabilisation force in order to provide security in a given area and the civilian-related factors would be dealt with by international and national aid agencies. However, this view is simplistic and over-optimistic, as experience has demonstrated that the military simply cannot divorce itself from civil considerations especially during humanitarian operations. The civil impacts on the military operation and vice versa have to be recognised and dealt with effectively for such missions to be fully successful.

In *The Path to Leadership*, Field Marshal Montgomery stated: 'The soldier and the politician have got to learn to understand each other; this is essential for the conduct of modern war. Too often each is liable to disregard or underrate the other's difficulties' (Montgomery, 1961). Since current operational environments have become increasingly complex with the military being just one of many actors in a murky pool of national and international agencies, Montgomery's statement is even more valid today than it was in 1961. Figure 6.3 highlights some of the agencies

FIGURE 6.3. Unity of effort?[4]

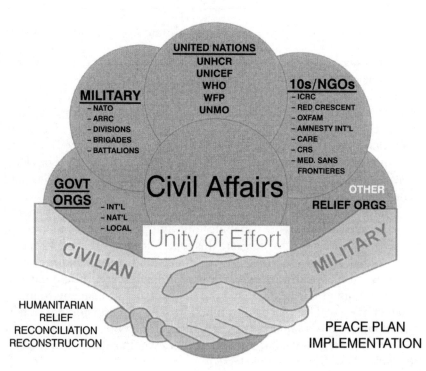

the military can expect to encounter when deployed operationally. This complex network requires a degree of interagency understanding and cooperation that often overstretches the capability of many military organisations.

Often there is a lack of understanding of what Civil Affairs entails and the skills military personnel require in order to be successful in this role. Furthermore, there is a need to determine who is going to undertake Civil Affairs duties and what level of training they require in order to operate effectively. It is arguable that on operational deployments, such as Bosnia-Herzegovina, Kosovo and East Timor, Civil Affairs should assume primacy in the military mission, after a secure environment has been created. This is based on the premise that at this stage most troops on the ground will become involved with Civil Affairs in some shape or form. The question is then, what form of instruction should soldiers receive in order to understand how their activities will affect the civilian and political dimensions of an operation and how the civil factors in turn affect the military mission?

It comes as a surprise to many that Civil Affairs is not a black art but is based upon principles of sound common sense gained from practical experience. Civil Affairs personnel need three sets of skills to facilitate military support to the political and civil mission. The relationship of these skill pillars to the building of military support for the civilian community is shown in Figure 6.4.

The first pillar has been called mission analysis, as it is essential that those involved in Civil Affairs understand how their role ties into their commander's mission and main effort. The British Army has a well-developed decision-making process called mission analysis and the US

FIGURE 6.4. The three pillars of Civil Affairs.[5]

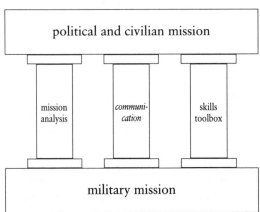

forces have a system called the military decision-making process. Essentially these tools have the same goal, which is to enable a subordinate to understand their tasks and any constraints in order to develop a coherent and integrated plan to support their military commander's mission. This is a key issue, as Civil Affairs personnel must never lose sight of the fact that they are working to support the military mission.

There is a second element to mission analysis, which is the need to develop an understanding of acceptable boundaries for Civil Affairs tasks, as personnel will often be operating outside of the normal sphere of military operations. This requires an ability to limit, focus and refine the processing of information and activities in support of the commander's stated main effort. If the work undertaken does not conform to this main effort, both the military and civilian audiences will dismiss Civil Affairs as irrelevant.

The second pillar represents a set of core skills that are required by Civil Affairs personnel in order to provide a 'toolbox' to support their role. The following list is not exhaustive and can be adapted to suit the operational requirements, but serves as a useful generic baseline:

- Working to key the principles of Civil Affairs such as transparency, honesty and avoiding dependency on the military by civilian agencies.

- How to conduct a Civil Affairs area assessment in order to gather and analyse pertinent information to support the mission.

- Understanding the organisation, structure and missions of civilian agencies in the operational area.

- Project management of Civil Affairs tasks.

- How to run Civil-Military cooperation centres in order that the military and civilian populations share important information effectively.

- Producing accurate, clear and succinct reports and returns for HQ staff and interested civilian agencies.

- Dealing with displaced person and refugee issues.

The central pillar from Figure 6.4 refers to communication, which is the key feature of the Civil Affairs capability. The ability to understand different organisational, societal and national cultures is critical to the success of communicating in a multinational and multi-organisational environment. The issue here is that there is no point in having a clear concept of the Civil Affairs mission and a fine toolbox of skills if the implications and consequences of any actions or decisions cannot be communicated effectively to both military and civilians.

In the past, poor communication with other organisations has led to a weakening of the military effort. Before the point is reached where a Civil Affairs operator is let loose on an unsuspecting world, he or she must have a good understanding of the principles of communication and how culture affects this process. Without this knowledge and the ability to apply it correctly, any other skills are at best ineffective and at worst dangerous. At one extreme, contemplation of the wrong end of a gun barrel is not the time to try to work out the likely cultural implication of any statement or gesture, as the learning curve might be short.

In 1996 Ambassador Holbrooke stated during an interview on his work in Bosnia-Herzegovina: 'You have to match your method to the moment and your style to the substance and the situation. And in this negotiation, dealing with people who are liars and in some cases killers, dealing with people who are desperate, dealing with traditions, you just have to get very tough' (Newshour, 1996).

There is clear recognition in Ambassador Holbrooke's statement of the importance of understanding other cultural perspectives and adapting one's approach to negotiating and communicating to best effect, even if this is unpalatable according to one's own set of values and beliefs. The importance of this practical viewpoint is reinforced by Edward T. Hall, a widely respected academic and business consultant in the field of cultural issues: 'Why bother to understand, to emphasise, to learn somebody else's culture? … we must be willing to admit that people of this planet don't just live in one world but in many worlds and some of these worlds, if not properly understood, can and do annihilate the others' (Hall, 1983).

So what exactly is culture and how can it be defined? Professor Geert Hofstede, one of the most renowned experts in this field, attempts to define culture as 'collective programming of the mind' (Hofstede, 1980). This collective programming lies between the universal nature of the human animal and an individual's unique personality. These three elements combine to provide the mental programming, which together make humans the social animals they are. These three levels are summarised in Figure 6.5. Hofstede states that 'Culture is to human collectivity what personality is to an individual' (Hofstede, 1980). Personality makes a human being truly unique through individual learning and inherited values, whereas culture determines the characteristics of a social grouping. It is these characteristics of social grouping that should interest Civil Affairs personnel.

Another perspective of culture is proposed by Dr Fons Trompenaars who is a recognised world leader in business communications: 'Culture is the way in which a group of people solves problems and reconciles dilemmas' (Trompenaars and Hampden-Turner, 1998). He also states that culture can be identified at different levels. The highest level is national

FIGURE 6.5. Three levels of mental programming.[6]

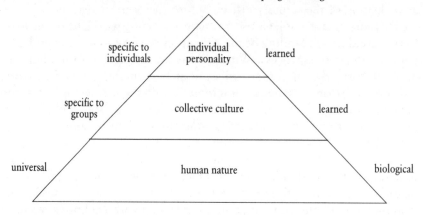

or regional culture. The manner in which attitudes are expressed within an organisation is the corporate culture. Individuals with certain functions, such as military personnel, will also have their own professional culture. The point of this statement is that there are different levels of cultural influence that may need to be observed by Civil Affairs operators in order to understand the perspective of an individual with whom one is trying to communicate.

There is a lot of discussion and little agreement among academics and practitioners over the precise nature of culture and how it should be defined. Paul Bohannan believes that 'Defining culture has proved all but impossible. Yet we know what culture is, just as we know what life and matter are. All three are what we might call rock-bottom perceptions – they cannot be definitionally simplified' (Bohannan, 1995). In spite of this there is a reasonable amount of agreement that the elements in Figure 6.6 are an acceptable basis for discussion, particularly the last one.

Having attempted to identify what form a culture might take, the next step for a Civil Affairs operator is to accept that an ethnocentric approach to communication and negotiation is not going to help the process. Ethnocentrism can be defined as an 'exaggerated tendency to think the characteristics of one's own group or race superior to those of other groups or races' (Drever, 1952). While most will accept that this is not conducive to effective communication, they find it hard to understand that people from other backgrounds are not going to see a given set of circumstances from the same perspective. Perspectives vary, but will be based upon the mental programming, i.e. the values and norms[8] of the social and work environment of the individual they are trying to communicate with and also their objectives. An important aside here, is

FIGURE 6.6. What culture is and what it is not.[7]

Culture is:
1. a shared system of meanings, which guides how the world is perceived
2. relative as there is no cultural absolute
3. learned in that it is derived from an individual's social environment
4. about groups as it is a collective phenomenon.

Culture is not:
1. right or wrong
2. genetically inherited
3. about individual behaviour
4. easy to understand.

that Civil Affairs operators must be careful how they are perceived by the outside world. The perception they create will become reality in the minds of the people with whom they are trying to communicate.

Two examples serve to demonstrate the impact of culture and the importance of perception. When conducting joint security operations there are basic differences in approach to duty that can cause tension between the British civil police and the British soldier on the ground. A police officer is trained to preserve life and property, whereas a soldier's training will lead him or her to try to close with and arrest a terrorist. Both approaches are inherently based on the organisations' different 'corporate' cultures and the training received. An understanding of each other's role and perspective should in most cases lead to a reduction in mistrust and a closer working relationship.

After the military operation in Haiti, members of the local population were interviewed concerning the role of the various military forces. The Canadians were perceived to have thoroughly understood the local culture, in part helped by the ability of many soldiers to speak French. They were, however, viewed as ineffective as there were 'no go' areas in which they would not operate. The Pakistanis were very much constrained by language and cultural differences and did not integrate well with the local population, but were treated with respect as they operated with apparent unconcern in the heart of dangerous areas. The will of the US Marine Corps was severely tested by local factions. The Marines' swift and robust response to early events helped to diffuse a potentially volatile situation and provided them with credibility in the eyes of the local population (Fitzgerald, 1999).

The second example shows that the military can have varied responses when operating under similar conditions and to the same of rules, and that the importance of cultural influence cannot be discounted. It is reasonable for a civilian to assume that the military in these circumstances would have a unified response to major incidents. This is not always the case and, in turn, a Civil Affairs operator should not expect individuals from a diverse range of humanitarian aid agencies, local civil authorities and local civilians to all have the same cultural perspective of events. This is why it is important for Civil Affairs personnel to understand 'culture' and how it affects the communication and negotiation processes.

The ability to communicate accurately, succinctly and unambiguously has been shown to be central to the Civil Affairs role. It needs to be understood by Civil Affairs personnel that both military and civilians are likely to view them with suspicion, unless they effectively articulate appropriate ideas and requirements. Therefore, the skills columns identified in Figure 6.4 provide the essential minimum training for those in the Civil Affairs role. A military commander and his or her staff are going to have many issues requiring their attention and will not have the inclination or energy to try and discern what it is a Civil Affairs operator is trying to tell them, unless the message is clearly and effectively received. This is particularly true when the message is unwelcome, unexpected or outside the normal sphere of military thought. On the other hand a message is unlikely to be well received by civilians if it is couched in unfamiliar military terminology and delivered with the insensitivity and ignorance that service personnel often display.

It has not been the purpose of this discussion to argue that any one military organisation should focus more closely on Civil Affairs. However, it is increasingly becoming a required military capability and, as already stated, is often not much more than the application of common sense and understanding. What is difficult, is to recognise and accept that civilian and political organisations will have differing sets of priorities and agendas, which may be in direct conflict with those of the military. It is the role of Civil Affairs to attempt to de-conflict these differences and achieve a relatively harmonious approach towards a given mission.

The goal of this discussion has been to raise what is essentially an issue of communication that is becoming increasingly important for military commanders to understand. It is accepted by most that it is incumbent upon a commander to ensure that his or her staff and troops are adequately trained to deal with the challenges they will face when on operational deployments. Therefore the three columns of Civil Affairs skills should be included with other essential pre-deployment training where applicable. It is suggested that the first month of a military operation is not the time to undertake 'on the job' training for Civil Affairs, as has often been the case in the past. The potential stakes in terms of human suffering and damage to the common mission are likely to be too high to be acceptable.

NOTES

1. Amended from Lieutenant-Colonel A.D. Wilson, Commanding Officer of the British Army Civil Affairs Group.
2. Lieutenant-Colonel A.D. Wilson.
3. Civil Affairs is a national term for this activity. NATO refers to Civil Affairs as Civil Military Cooperation (CIMIC).
4. Lieutenant-Colonel A.D. Wilson.
5. Amended from Colonel M. Hess, Deputy Commander US Army 353rd Civil Affairs Command, New York.
6. Major A.B. Stocker, British Army Civil Affairs Group (adapted from Hofstede, 1980; and Hoecklin, 1995).
7. Adapted from Hoecklin, 1995.
8. *Values* are the assumptions social groupings use to deal with a given situation, usually subconsciously. *Norms* are accepted behaviour such as dress-codes and methods of addressing others.

REFERENCES

Bohannan, P. (1995), *How Culture Works* (New York: Free Press).
Drever, J. (1952), *A Dictionary of Psychology* (Harmondsworth: Penguin).
Fitzgerald, A. (1999), interview, Cranfield University, Royal Military College of Science.
Hall, E.T. (1983), *The Dance of Life: The Other Dimension of Time* (New York: Anchor Press/Doubleday).
Hoecklin, L. (1995), *Managing Cultural Differences: Strategies for Competitive Advantage* (Harlow: Addison Wesley Longman).
Hofstede, G. (1980), *Culture's Consequences: International Differences in Work-related Values* (Beverley Hills, CA: Sage).
Montgomery, Viscount (1961), *The Path to Leadership* (London: Collins).
Morgan, L.G.S.F. (1950), *Overture to Overlord* (Garden City, NY: Doubleday).
Newshour (1996), 'Making Peace', PBS Online.
Spybey, T. (1996), *Globalization and World Society* (Cambridge: Polity Press).
Trompenaars, F. and Hampden-Turner, C. (1998), *Riding the Waves of Culture: Understanding Cultural Diversity in Business* (New York: McGraw Hill).

7

Constructing Truth: Understanding the Role of Information and Mediation within Military Affairs

SUSAN C. DRISCOLL

INTRODUCTION

All the world's a stage, and all the men and woman merely players ...
(William Shakespeare, *As You Like It*).

In this age of information and communication the metaphor of the world as a stage has never been more appropriate. The proliferation of the media and specifically that of computer-mediated communication has led to an era of armchair activism and global observation never before experienced. Events have become the concern of the masses, rather than solely the business of the privileged or ultimately responsible few. The ability to receive and share information globally has created societies wherein actor and audience become one. To observe is to be a part. As such, events have become boundless, determined not by the details of what actually occurs but by the way in which they are mediated, received and interpreted. Aided by rapid technological development, this endless cycle has led our world to be characterised as kaleidoscopic, deriving its shifting form from those who play and those who watch.

To refer to a 'theatre' of operation provides a useful description of events within the military context, but 'theatre' does not assume some form of passive observation. As a result of the information age, those observing a conflict have become actively drawn on to the stage. Conflicts have expanded to encompass the machinations of the public. The battlefield, thus, becomes an issue of battlespace (Alberts, 1999) enveloping those who have become caught up in the perpetual transmittance of information and whose actions become influenced by what they receive.

Information has been recognised as an empowering source and as an asset that allows one person to have superiority over another. However, having access to, or being subject to, information does not necessarily equate to greater knowledge or clarity. Clausewitz (1988) refers to the *fog* of war as a lack of common awareness, the inability to assemble knowledge and existing information. Such fog is as likely to thicken in information age as it is to clear. The potential for confusion, misinformation and differences in perception are vast when one considers the complexity that the information age brings. As such, increased information has the potential to bring about *friction* (Clausewitz, 1988), encumbrance and misperception, just as much as it is likely to provide shared situational awareness and collaboration.

Superiority, whether military or commercial, relies not only on recognising the critical function that information serves but on understanding the requirement for information to be managed. Information with no structure is analogous to a play that has no director: it becomes a meaningless turn of events. Therefore, just as a play requires direction and stage-management, so military operations require *information management* for them to succeed. As Campbell (1999) states: 'In this changed media environment, in a modern conflict, particularly one fought by an alliance of nations, with different politics, different military systems and different histories, effective communications is not merely a legitimate function; it is an essential one.'

As the information environment changes, so the military role assumes new responsibilities. The challenges facing the military in modern society circle around the increasing occurrence of Operations Other than War (OOTW). The global perception of the military has changed to encompass war-fighter, peacekeeper and humanitarian relief worker. For the military, it is critical that these roles and intentions are well communicated, not just to a potential adversary, but also to foreign and home populations.

While the military do attempt to communicate their message, the rapid and vastly interconnected technology of the information age affords the opportunity for many others to do the same. The reality of war is translated into an *image*, or perception, of war, and it is this that is disseminated through the media at large. The possibility for variation within the communication of one issue is considerable and is aided further by the means through which the information can be mediated. Television, radio, print journalism, the internet and, traditionally, word-of-mouth all provide vehicles for communicating messages to home populations throughout the world. *Fact* merges into story-telling and *truth* is reconstructed through an attempt to decipher and interpret information which has become diluted in a sea of mass communication.

Just as we encounter a military war, we also experience a media or information war. Yet the two are in fact incompatible. Our understanding or perceptual experience of a war, conflict or humanitarian crisis is driven by a subjective assemblage of the information we receive. Our knowledge or experience, unless encountered firsthand, is always subject to mediation and, thus, is characterised purely as a *perception* – a subjective conglomerate of information leading to a transient and often mutable understanding of events.

The importance of constructing the 'right' perception becomes obvious. The perception of reality matters as much as reality itself. The development of the information age expedites this further, allowing for direct and powerful images and events to be communicated through a variety of media. Although this is not necessarily new phenomenon (Taylor, 1992), advancements in communication technology have exacerbated this potential to the point where information superiority, either as the collection of information or through its dissemination, becomes a critical priority during times of conflict.

Information globalisation has led to a re-emergence of military capabilities specifically designed to tackle the concept of information operations and provide information support. Information operations reflects the vast range of command, technical and psychological issues which are made more prominent by information globalisation and which need to be designed to work in support of traditional command structures in order to become a *force multiplier and combat reducer*. Information operations encompasses command and control warfare (which itself includes psychological operations (Psyops) or information support) as well as Civil Affairs and media operations. Despite apparent differences between these capabilities, the ways and means of achieving their operational aims are not mutually exclusive. The success of any campaign, whether this is an operational campaign to deploy peacekeeping troops in the local community, a media campaign to release particular news stories to press agencies, or a psychological campaign specifically targeting the attitudes of non-combatants, relies on influencing *perceptions*. Both the term 'perceptions' and the expression 'hearts and minds' (an emotive term often used to refer to perceptions) will now be discussed in more detail.

PERCEPTIONS

'Perception' has become a fashionable phrase, frequently used to define the *socio*-cognitive notion of sense-making and understanding. Current interest has arisen as a result of numerous societal developments such as consumerism, global media and a greater demand for instantly informing and constantly updated news. However, 'perception' is a term that opens conversation as quickly in some circles as it closes them in others. To discuss methods by which to influence someone's perception is often regarded as an anathema within a democratic society, and yet every year millions are poured into managing the 'perception' (or more acceptably termed the 'image') of political parties, organisations and industries. It is unfortunate that due to the 'propaganda' tactics used in the First and Second World Wars, and during conflicts since, information operations (especially psychological operations) has rather ironically fallen victim to the effects of a badly managed perception.

Recently, however, military capabilities such as Psyops, or information support, have been proven to play a critical and legitimate role within operations. The concerns which condemned any practice that involved influence or persuasion through direct targeting (despite the fact that traditional methods of attrition do exactly this) were undermined during the Balkan crisis in 1995, when the UK took decisive action to deploy the UK Psyops group to support the information campaign within Bosnia. 'These concerns ... had bedevilled the effective use of the capability for many years, and this was almost certainly a reason for its non-use to support any UN military peacekeeping operations since 1945' (Stone, 1997).

The nature of warfare is being redefined and, so too, are the means to fight it. The information age, to echo the words of Sun Tsu (500 BC), provides a further means to 'break the enemy's resistance without fighting'. To understand how supremacy can be achieved in such a way one must be able to appreciate the reasons why the use of information during conflicts can be successful and powerful and why, most importantly, they are in need of control.

PERCEPTIONS OF CONFLICTS

Since the press were given unlimited access during the Vietnam War, there has remained great sensitivity to the issue of who is reporting what to whom. During both the Falklands War and the Gulf War better attempts were made to control the flow of information to foreign and home populations. However, despite similar efforts in 1999, the Kosovo crisis again showed that achieving the right perception can bring a force closer to winning a battle.

Conflicts which occur in relatively sophisticated societies such as Serbia provide an interesting example of the information battle. Unlike many Third World countries which experience conflicts and civil wars, Serbia's access to modern communication technology such as the internet meant that in 1999 the West was matched in terms of its ability to mediate information both nationally and abroad. For the media, therefore, the Kosovo crisis became a race for information supremacy. As the UK prime minister's press secretary stated:

> That NATO could win militarily was never really in doubt. The only battle we might lose was the battle for hearts and minds. The consequence would have been NATO ending the bombing and losing the war. Keeping public support, keeping the Alliance united and showing Milosevic we were united, was what we were all about (Campbell, 1999).

Serbia's 'law on information' brought about the closure of many of that country's independent media, whilst the Serbian government continued to maintain a firm grip on information. Tanjug, Milosevic's news agency, continued to feed a steady diet of pro-government, anti-NATO information to the people of Serbia, whilst the free press within the Western media were desperately trying to get hold of any information available to them in order to meet their agendas. However, the restrictions on the Western press within Belgrade and Kosovo meant that little news was coming out, and that which did usually served only to add further credence to the line being pushed by Serbia's more nationalistic media. So, whilst emotive images of dying children and burning embassies confronted the people of Serbia, the West was left with little more than images of precision bombings and formal briefings given from behind podiums by token military speakers, politicians or NATO spokesmen.

Despite the 'facts' of the situation, for many (especially the Serbs) the perception of what was happening and why were quite different. Serbia's Ministry for Information had managed a well-orchestrated information campaign which, through omission, deception and fact had exploited the very mechanisms which form perceptions. Information was consistent: it lacked, through careful omission and censoring, any inconsistencies. It was cohesive because many people began to seek and filter information for themselves, and it relied on powerful imagery to capture the population's attention and convey its message rapidly and emotively. Thus, a story was set in place which apparently encompassed the whole picture. There was little need for people to make sense of it themselves as the story had been pieced together already. Others, however, did try to seek out a different story, buying satellite antennae in the hope of receiving CNN or Radio Free Europe. However, for many a particular construction of the 'truth' had been accepted: hearts and minds in Serbia, to a large extent, had been won.

For the West the story was, literally, quite different. With the accessibility of so much information through television, radio, newspapers and the internet we were afforded our democratic right to construct our own perceptions. However, for many 'Kosovo' had been created from a mixture of briefly glimpsed news headlines and attempts to watch briefings accompanied by re-runs of daily strategic bombings. Further, as is often the case during war, reporting accuracy and coordination were over-ridden by immediacy (Wentz, 1997). As a result the majority of the population within the UK were left trying to construct the 'truth' from a medley of relatively inconsistent, incoherent and impassive news bulletins; perceptions emerged based not on a coherent story but on disparate, incomplete facts. Perceptions were thus fragmented; hearts were saying one thing, whilst minds were saying something quite different.

HEARTS AND MINDS

What do such comparisons teach us? Perhaps the most important and obvious lesson is that information is a critical component of military operations and, further, whoever maintains control of it is likely to benefit militarily. As technology develops and begins to encompass the currently underdeveloped areas around the globe, the information factor becomes all the more important.

The term 'hearts and minds' is often used to refer to the influence that perceptions, or particular information, can have over the decisions we make, the way we think or the way we chose to act. This is an issue of concern not only to those in the media world but it has been also recognised by the military for its powerful potential. Information has become a much-sought-after commodity, both for those who wish to be informed and for those who wish to be the informers.

Marketeers, media moguls and advertisers alike have become only too aware of the way in which their audiences use information. Further to this, the proliferation and pervasiveness of global communications has meant that audiences have become much easier to profile and to target with information. The result is an exploitation of opportunities through the media to reach the *hearts and minds* of the public at large, achieved through strategies that will be discussed in the next section.

News-reporting is a critical element of this hearts and minds issue. However, as a form of mediated information, the impact of news-reporting on the receiver is not straightforward. Robinson and Levy

(1986, cited in Livingstone, 1998) found that viewers understood only one-third of news stories, especially when such stories were of political interest. Livingstone (1998) attributes this to the difficulty in addressing the average viewers in terms of 'those for whom news discourse is jargon, those for whom world geography is hazy, or for whom political details are boring'.

Across the globe, therefore, the battle for hearts and minds is fought not just between adversaries but also within alliances. The stakes are raised as the battle is waged for both information superiority *and* ratings.

Most of the research into issues relating to the information age has tended to focus on keeping pace with technological advancements and identifying the impact that information can have on critical, technological information systems (communication networks, the internet, television news, finance, power distribution, etc.). Far less attention has been paid to understanding the human as one of the most significant elements within the information network. As a result, there has been a general failure to recognise that the impact of information is as much about the need to understand *the interpretative role of the user* as it is about the information itself.

The next two sections begin to address this apparent lack of attention. To maintain focus, a definition of perception will be explored, using Boyd's terms *observation* and *orientation* (1984, cited in Allard, 1996) to help clarify the process of information dissemination and reception. Observation will be used to examine the impact that information can have upon a target audience, specifically using the medium of images, and orientation will afford an assessment of what the audience brings to the information in the form of interpretation and sense-making. Boyd's original use of the OODA loop was developed to illustrate the decision-making cycle – Observe, Orientate, Decide and Act. This was designed to show that the aim of any conflict strategy (and this was subsequently deemed especially relevant to command and control warfare) was to get inside the tactical decision-making loop of one's adversary. Through this one could either degrade their ability to process information, by disrupting one of the stages, or, by forcing the decision-making process to cycle too quickly so that an adversary could not cope with the demands being made, render their command and control inefficient (Allard, 1996).

The Boyd model provides a useful framework from which to work, although here the terms observation and orientation will only be used tentatively. The decision-making process is complex, as are the initial stages of observation and orientation. There is no clear differentiation between information that exists *outside* of the human mind and that which has been observed and taken *inside* the mind to be processed. We attend to information continuously; the mind is rarely shut off from processing the world around it. Both the social world and cognitive world are mutually affecting and interactive and not to be regarded as totally distinct mechanical elements.

OBSERVATION

To qualify this last statement, a definition of observation is proposed. Observation refers to the attention towards a particular experience either visually, aurally, emotionally or through any other sense. It is similar to the traditional meaning of taking *notice* of something. However, in this instance the term will be used specifically to refer to the 'something' being communicated as *information*, that is, information designed to be observed and to bring about some form of effect.

Specifically, images will be used as an example of mediated information. By examining the way in which images can be constructed to convey particular meanings and messages, much can be learned about how information generally is actively received by its audience.

With the increase of communication in everyday society, images have developed to serve an important function within society. Images provide a means of conveying huge amounts of information to an audience in a very short amount of time. Deutsch (1997) states that images provide us with a 'condensed version of events'. He continues that as the 'information highway' gathers speed it becomes impossible to keep pace with what is happening around us; therefore, we need to be brought up to date, to feed our understanding and help build our mental picture of what is occurring in and around our world. 'In an ever changing society what we look for and quite often what we see is information which provides an instant definition of the world around us ... we are constantly looking to define the shape that our society is taking ... change is ever present' (Deutsch, 1997).

In this media age, definition of meaning matters even more. The possibility of being swamped by information is counteracted by images that present information to us in an intelligible and meaningful form. Quite often it is the lack of images that draws our attention to their importance as a form of communication. Certainly within the Kosovo crisis in 1999, the lack of pictures from the Balkans has been pinpointed as causing a communication problem between NATO and the Serbian and home populations during the conflict. Campbell (1999) made this clear when he stated that 'there is a real problem ... namely: no images, no news'.

Images, therefore, have become a powerful commodity, serving not only as an effective means of communication but as a shaper of perceptions. They are often the vehicle for particular perspectives, biases and ideologies to be carried forward into society and, when a particularly powerful image is used, its effects on an audience can be quite dramatic. One only has to consider the powerful connotations conveyed by a swastika or even by the images of dictators such as Saddam Hussein or Slobodan Milosevic to realise how we have come to associate particular values with such images. The importance of observation, therefore, lies in understanding how it is that images come to mean different things and, especially in this era of global mediation, how one can start to anticipate why some images become more powerful than others. According to Deutsch (1997), to understand how images work we must examine the way in which the mind transforms such portrayals into culturally and personally meaningful objects.

SEMIOTICS

One key way in which this examination can be conducted is through semiotics. In its most basic form, semiotics refers to the study of signs. It is an approach that allows one to break down a sign or image into its component parts, or codes, in order to look at how meaning is created. Codes in this context refer to those pieces of information which hold particular shared meanings for their audience and which, when coupled with other codes and placed in particular contexts, convey a particular discourse, ideology or simply an idea. The most straightforward example of this most basic description of semiotics is to consider a military uniform. A military uniform is an image. As an image or a sign, a uniform is constructed from various codes. The codes are the symbols and decorations on that uniform, in the form of pips, stripes, medals or badges. To one who knows what these codes mean, they will *observe* the uniform in order to make sense of who a particular person is, what service they are from and what rank they hold. In this case, they are *reading* the image before them. A perception begins to be formed which will in turn influence a belief about what this person may be like and perhaps how one should tailor one's own behaviour in his or her presence.

Traditionally, according to Sassure (1915, as cited in Chandler, 1997), images or signs can be broken down into three elements: the signifier, the signified and sense (Sturrock, 1986). The signifier refers to the thing itself, the denotative object that we observe, for example, the military uniform – the jacket and trousers with badges and stripes. Secondly, there is what

106

is signified by the signifier, for example, three pips meaning captain or a particular medal reflecting 'service in Northern Ireland'. We have existing perceptions of what it means to be a captain or to have served in Northern Ireland, and these are the connotations: shared understandings or common meanings held by those within a particular culture. Finally, there is the third element of the sign – sense. This refers to our own personal interpretation of what the sign or codes mean. For example, the interpretation of a medal for serving in Northern Ireland will be quite different depending on one's experience of that province. What such a medal may mean to a British Army officer may be quite different to the interpretation accorded it by a Catholic living in Londonderry.

We can begin to see how images have such an impact and are able to communicate so much information, often in so little space. However, how does semiotics assist our exploration of the information age when it implies that to anticipate the powerful effect of an image on a particular culture one must understand the meaning of every code and sign? In its traditional Sassurian form it is both inappropriate and unrewarding to even consider tackling this task: however, a development of semiotics theory does offer possibilities.

The problem in its Sassurian form is that codes and signs do not maintain fixed meanings but derive their meaning from the context in which they are placed, their assemblage with other information and, most importantly, the way in which they are *mediated*. For example, how does the meaning of what it is to 'serve in Northern Ireland' change when it is conveyed through the symbol of a medal as opposed to watching troops on the streets of Belfast on television news? Or, how does the significance of a medal change when it is displayed in a glass case and announced over the internet as opposed to being found lying in the street? Mediation refers to the means through which information is communicated and, as mediation and context change, so too does the meaning of the message. We can consider mediation and context to be forces acting upon information and giving it the potential to mean something to the viewer (Massumi, 1993). Attempting to determine the meaning of something should therefore not rely upon merely deconstructing the information alone but should also recognise the forces that are acting upon it. We can begin to understanding the *potential* that information has for developing particular meanings at particular points in time, thus allowing for the dynamic and polysemic nature of information to be characterised.

To consider and attempt to characterise exactly what the forces are that shape our perceptions brings this discussion closer to the notion of orientation. Force of meaning is not a one-way flow from communicator to reader but two-way, with meaning determined as the two flows or forces converge. Therefore, important as it is to attempt to identify the indeterminate themes and discourses that information conveys, it is equally important to look at the force that the reader exercises upon the image in order to 'realise' its meaning (Eco, cited in Livingstone, 1998). As Iser (1980, cited in Livingstone, 1998) argues, the meaning of information cannot be determined by its content alone or by the reader who will receive it, but through a convergence of the two: 'It [information, 'text'] must inevitably be virtual in character, as it cannot be reduced to the reality of the text or to the subjectivity of the reader, and it is from this virtuality that it derives its dynamism.'

There has been a move towards developing the relationship between theories of information (or text) and those of readers (Livingstone, 1998). A key concern remains the actual contribution that the viewer makes to the negotiation of meaning. In the following section we will move away from what we observe, what the information *is* in the form of images codes and signs, towards looking at what people, as viewers, actively *do* with this information.

ORIENTATION

It has become necessary to examine how the audience actually selects, perceives, decodes and makes sense of media texts (Schroder, 1987, cited in Livingstone, 1998).

Meanings are not given prior to interpretation (Livingstone, 1998).

Many of the models of media effects either address the audience as passive, uncritical and homogenous or have developed theories which offer little consideration of the audience as an active component of the mediation process. Conversely, other theories reject the impact of powerful media effects in the quest for a purely constructionist view of audience interpretation. However, if we consider information (an image or text) from the 'role of the reader' (Eco, 1979, cited in Livingstone, 1998) an understanding begins to develop which allows the importance, and force, of both the text and the reader to be taken into consideration.

I propose to use the term 'orientation' as referring to the sense-making that occurs once information has been observed. It is the sorting, organising and forming of meaning that allows one to achieve an understanding, or perception, of events. According to Eco (1987, cited in Capozzi, 1997), information is often open to interpretation and as a result its meaning is *emergent*. However, this is not to deny that information has a structuring role as much as the viewer has a constructive role. The interesting issue is that the potential effect of the original piece of information or message can be transformed depending on who is receiving it. For example, if an event occurs during a conflict, such as a hospital being bombed, the information from this event will be selected, filtered and constructed into a news story. This news story will then be broadcast to an audience who, in turn will also select, filter and interpret the meaning and in their own way make sense of what happened. Thus the meaning has emerged over time and through mediation and, just as the event or news story is structured, so the original is transformed as the receiver constructs his or her own perception of that event. The question is, what particular features of what is called social-cognition drive this construction process?

Mental images, or perceptions, begin to form as we attempt to construct a consistent and meaningful conceptualisation of events. They reflect the viewer's understanding and awareness of an event as it currently stands and are used to generate future expectations. According to Livingstone (1988) the result is a Gestalt: a configuration of parts that together create a meaningful whole (Reber, 1985). In this sense, however, the Gestalt is never fully crystallised due to its dynamic and mutable nature. However, using the notion of a perceptual Gestalt allows us to characterise exactly what orientation involves.

One of the critical principles of Gestalt organisation is 'continuation' (Eysenck and Keane, 1994). This refers to the grouping of those elements requiring the fewest changes or interruptions. In orientation terms this means that information may be selected or filtered for its similarity and coherence with a pre-existing perception or other pieces of information. In this way perceptions can be likened to schemas which are defined as cognitive structures which represent knowledge about particular concepts (Fiske and Taylor, 1991). Schemas facilitate top–down processing – that is, where interpretation is determined by what the perceiver brings to the situation rather than what the situation presents to the perceiver. In much the same way perceptions, which many argue to be the same as schemas, manage this information tide in a similar way, in that new information is heavily filtered by prior knowledge. Once a particular perception begins to form towards (a political party for example) the assimilation of new information about that party will be strongly influenced by the perception that exists already. The reason for this is the cognitive requirement for continuation or, in information terms, *narrative*.

Narrative is the consistency that allows us to form expectations and make inferences about events that may occur in the future. It drives interpretation and comprehension so that the perception we construct maintains a meaningful structure that contains few if any inconsistencies. Technically, we become the storytellers. We begin to construct our own version of events according to the information we receive and actively select. Our expectations drive our perception of new events and we begin to form a story, filling in gaps and elaborating on information in order that it 'fits' with our 'story so far'. Therefore, as narrative drives the story along, the meaning begins to emerge.

Characterising the process of orientation is rather like being a co-author of a book. Just as we observe news stories and read papers, much of the information is already structured; yet it is our decision either to accept the 'first draft' or to rearrange the pages and chapters in order to form a better story. However, our story is being constructed from many sources so when new 'chapters' or 'pages' come along, it is necessary that they are made to fit with the existing story-line, either through accepting the information, adapting the contents to give new meaning, or disregarding it entirely. Using such a metaphor to consider how perceptions work we can argue that we have many 'books' and stories, each continuing to develop, evolve and change over time.

So what happens when inconsistencies do arise in our stories and, despite attempts to disregard or change the meaning of new information, our expectations are not met? Such a situation causes surprise and, often to a large extent, what is termed *cognitive dissonance* (Fiske and Taylor, 1991). The element of surprise works on the basis that it breaks down an individual's ability to anticipate or mentally prepare for a particular event to occur, thus causing confusion. The introduction of such disruptive material leads pre-existing perceptions related to the incident to be modified in line with the new 'facts' of the situation. In the same way as we construct the meaning in texts in the light of existing knowledge, we reconstruct our pre-existing perception when the information is irrefutable. For example, when we read a book only to find the hero to be the villain in the final chapter, we find ourselves re-evaluating the behaviour of the hero/villain in the previous chapters in the light of the new information. Often, when we cannot change the facts, we have to deal with the information by realigning our narrative structure. Snyder and Uranowitz (1978, cited in Livingstone, 1998) illustrate this process in their findings that people's memory of a particular narrative was radically altered when the central character was subsequently said to be a lesbian.

A second Gestalt principle which complements that of consistency, is closure. This refers to the way that we actively fill in any missing parts of the information in order to form a meaningful whole. Thus, assumptions and inferences are our attempts to fill the gaps that information has not yet provided. Just as visually we will see a circle even if it is an incomplete curved line, so we also form perceptions about events or people on the basis of insubstantial information. As Deutsch (1997a) puts it: 'We take those things that stand out and make them fit with what we already know, want and expect ... we assume consistency with what might yet come, complacently fill in any blanks and concoct an image.' The inferences we might make about the following story illustrate this process:

> A man came around a street corner holding a gun in both hands when a soldier appeared and demanded he put down his weapon. A shot was fired and the soldier fell to the ground. The man turned and quickly ran away.

Consider the inferences you have made about this short story and the characters within it. The preferred reading leads us to assume that 'the man' is perhaps some sort of terrorist. We assume that because we are aware that the man is carrying the gun and has been asked to put it down by a soldier who we (also) assume to be acting in an official capacity. We are further led to believe that the shot fired came from the man and was aimed at the soldier. However, we do not know that the man is guilty and the soldier innocent – or that the man fired the shot – or that the soldier was hit. The shot could have come from a third party causing the soldier to drop to the ground for cover and the man to turn and run. Many inferences can be generated and used in order to impose some form of consistency upon the story we have been given. As Deutsch stated, what we have done is to 'complacently fill in any blanks' in order to 'concoct an image'.

In summary, orientation can be characterised as an attempt actively to seek confirmatory rather than falsifying evidence in order to confirm our existing perceptions. Further, our need for cognitive consistency illustrates how influential the viewer or audience is in the process of constructing their own personal meanings and understandings of the world around them. The result for the viewer, therefore, is the formation of cohesive and orderly perception that potentially offers some form of sanctuary from the unrelenting penetration of mass communications into our everyday lives.

CONCLUSION

Information has been recognised as an empowering source: an asset which allows one to have superiority over others, but (as we have seen) this is only so if it is used in a coordinated and consistent manner. For the viewer to form a perception in the presence of a perpetual flood of disarrayed and often contradictory information is not an easy task. It becomes possible only through our necessity to ignore or to actively seek information in order to impose consistency. However, our perceptions of the world are not static but kaleidoscopic. Sense emerges briefly only to change again as perceptions are shaken up, causing new meanings and understandings to take form.

Our appreciation of the role of information in this way must evolve to encompass military affairs if we hope to meet the challenges that are manifest in the information age. We must ensure a balance of interest between both technology and the human; otherwise too much focus on technology may lead us to find that neglect of the human component has led to a deficient understanding of the new role information-users play. Already a plethora of significant new players has emerged, who have not only become critical observers but who are also empowered by information and thus actively involved.

It has become necessary to characterise the role of these new information-users both in relation to technology and to globalisation as a whole, and to recognise them as significant and influential elements within all information networks. The aim of such a challenge, therefore, should be to appreciate information in its dynamic form; account for its polymorphic nature; consider the way in which information is mediated; identify the likely audience who will receive it; and most importantly of all, to anticipate the perception that may emerge from it.

NOTE

This work was carried out as part of Technology Group 5 of the MoD Corporate Research Programme. The views expressed within this paper are those of the author and do not represent an official DERA position. It is published by permission of DERA on behalf of the controller, HMSO.

REFERENCES

Alberts, D. (1999), 'Network Centric Warfare', available at *http://www.dodccrp. org/NCW/imply_mil_ops.htm*.

Allard, K. (1996), *Command Control and Common Defence* (revd edn; New Haven, CT: Yale University Press, National Defence University, Institute for National and Strategic Studies).

Campbell, A. (1999), 'Kosovo: Communications Lessons for Nato, the Military and the Media' (speech at the Royal United Services Institute, London).

Chandler, D. (1997), 'Semiotics for Beginners', available at *wysiwg://59/http:// www.aber.ac. uk/~dgc/sem01.html*.

Clausewitz, C. von (1988), *On War* (New York: Viking Penguin).

Capozzi, R. (ed.) (1997), *Reading Eco: An Anthology* (Bloomington, IL, and Indianapolis, IN: Indiana University Press).

Deutsch, R.D. (1997a), 'Probing Images of Politicians and International Affairs', DERA Contract Report (unpublished).

—— (1997b), 'Minding Princess Di', *Slate Magazine*.

Eysenck, M.W. and Keane, M.T. (1994), *Cognitive Psychology: A Student's Handbook* (London: LEA).

Fiske, S.T. and Taylor, S.E. (1991), *Social Cognition* (2nd edn; Singapore: McGraw-Hill international eds).

Livingstone, S. (1998), *Making Sense of Television: The Psychology of Audience Interpretation* (2nd edn; London: Routledge).

Massumi, B. (1993), *A User's Guide to Capitalism and Schizophrenia: Deviations from Deleuze and Gauttari* (Cambridge, MA: MIT Press).

Reber, A.S. (1985), *Dictionary of Psychology* (Harmondsworth: Penguin).

Stone, D.J.A. (1997), 'Out of the Shadows ... The Re-emergence of the UK's Military Psychological Operations Capability since 1945', *British Army Review*, 114, pp. 3–12.

Sturrock, J. (1986), *Movements and Ideas: Structuralism* (London: Paladin/ Grafton).

Taylor, P.M. (1992), 'Propaganda from Thucydides to Thatcher: Some Problems, Perspectives and Pitfalls', opening address to the Social History Society of Great Britain's conference, available at *http://www.leeds.ac.uk/ics/arts-pt1.htm*.

Wentz, L. (ed.) (1997), *Lessons from Bosnia: The IFOR Experience* (Washington, DC: National Defence University, Institute National Strategic Studies).

PART 3
Seeking Frameworks

8

UNPROFOR: An Encounter without an Outcome

DEBORAH GOODWIN

INTRODUCTION: ESTABLISHING B-H COMMAND

The Bosnia-Herzegovina (B-H) Command mission to support UNHCR efforts to deliver humanitarian aid throughout Bosnia was neither a peacemaking nor peacekeeping operation, in the strict definitions of the terms. The Command was deployed at very short notice into a country with three warring factions and where no peace existed, with orders to fulfil a strictly humanitarian and limited political mission which had no strategic objective.

The advent of B-H Command heralded a change in UN policy for peacekeeping operations. The Command was formed in theatre in a very short period by some eight (subsequently ten) nations, the majority of which were providing and funding contingents (as opposed to individuals) and sharing the cost of the Command HQ. Such an arrangement for a peacekeeping operation was without UN precedence and, while operationally effective, led to a degree of independence of thought and action by the contributing nations. While in the early stages the effectiveness of HQ B-H Command stemmed largely from its formation from the core of an existing NATO HQ, the slow implementation of a financial basis caused immense problems and affected operational efficiency.

The Command was formed in order to support UNHCR in delivering humanitarian aid throughout Bosnia-Herzegovina. The force was to be at 'no cost to the United Nations'. Against this background the contributing nations met in London (the UK took on the responsibility of lead nation) and agreed force contributions. The headquarters was based on a NATO HQ style with additional staff from the contributing nations, plus communications from the Netherlands and the HQ support from Denmark. The proposed structure was forwarded to the UN in New York on 20 September 1992 and subsequently approved. Security Resolution 776 was adopted on 14 September 1992 and B-H Command was complete in theatre by mid November 1992 – a period of two months. This was probably all accomplished as swiftly as could reasonably be expected, given the need for national contingents to be self-sufficient.

The mandate for UNPROFOR in Bosnia-Herzegovina was significantly different from that for UNPROFOR in Croatia. With time, the Command had taken on far wider responsibilities than those originally envisaged in the mandate, including peacemaking on the ground, negotiating and monitoring ceasefires, delivering aid in areas too dangerous for UNHCR to enter, assisting refugees and displaced persons, arranging exchanges of prisoners and bodies, and escorting utility repair missions. The ability to react rapidly to take advantage of the local situation, both political and operational, is essential and the HQ structure had to be adjusted accordingly.

The selection of troops was a matter for the contributing nations once the political declarations had been made and initial reconnaissance conducted. Each contingent was responsible for its own logistic and administrative support and selected its force contribution to suit its area of operation. There was considerable variation in the size and equipment of each battalion group, particularly in regard to its combat and logistic support. Some units were able to rely on national support elements already in theatre to support the original UNPROFOR units.

The force was deployed in a very short space of time following the adoption of Security Council Resolution 776 on 14 September 1992. HQ B-H Command had a limited operational capability in Belgrade within a month and a skeleton HQ in Kiseljak, Bosnia-Herzegovina, a week later. It was not fully established, however, until the arrival of its HQ Support Company in early November 1992. By mid November 1992, all planned B-H Command units were in theatre.

A successful peacekeeping force must be supported by a proper political and military structure at all levels, with a clear strategic objective and an overall theatre commander responsible for controlling all agencies, both military and civilian. B-H Command was devised by the contributing nations on a purely military basis. It was appreciated that the Command was deploying into an area in which a three-sided civil war was in progress and that it had a clear mandate to support UNHCR. It quickly became apparent that the Command had to assume far wider responsibility, including political and military negotiations at the highest level between all three sides. The first Civil Affairs/Information Adviser arrived in late

November 1992, while the Civil Affairs Coordinator arrived in early January 1993, some three months into the operation, in spite of requests for a team from the outset. Prior to this, the commander of B-H Command, or his representative, had to negotiate with both political leaders and military commanders often without direct political advice.

The working language of English within the Command was an enormous advantage for the HQ as the core staff came from NATO headquarters, and thus both officers and soldiers were thoroughly familiar with the language. It was undoubtedly a problem for some other participating nations whose mother tongue was not English, and the speed with which the HQ had to work, particularly in the early stages, meant that there was little time for lengthy translations. It followed that in a multinational HQ it was deemed ideal if all personnel arrived with a sound working knowledge of the common language, to be effective in the short term as well as the long term. Although the situation was not quite the same in units which could operate in their own language for much of the time, there was an obvious requirement for radio traffic and communications between headquarters and units, and between units, to be in a common language. This also occurred at lower levels with, for example, convoy escorts needing to communicate with the convoys they were escorting.

The capabilities of the members of the staff of the HQ were affected by their ability in the common language, their experience in working in multinational headquarters and their familiarity with NATO procedures and methods of working in the HQ. Staff officers who had only national experience had more to learn than others, although this was generally only a problem in the early stages when the HQ was being established.

HQ B-H Command deployed with barely sufficient numbers of G5 (Civil Military Operations) and Public Information (PI) officers. The UN Chief of Press and Information arrived in the mission area in late November 1992 but left in mid January 1993. A successor was found only in March 1993, and it was some three months after deployment that professional UN Civil Affairs officers, suitable for conducting negotiations at national level, joined the HQ.[1]

A DUAL ROLE: PEACEKEEPING AND PEACEMAKING?

The clear lesson of Somalia and Bosnia is that to confuse the strategic goals of war fighting and peacekeeping will risk the mission and the very lives of the peacekeepers and aid workers themselves. A peacekeeping force designed to assist the delivery of humanitarian aid simply cannot be used to alter the military balance of force in a civil war, to modify political goals of one party or another, or even to attempt to enforce the passage of a convoy, for these are pure acts of war.[2]

This pertinent conclusion by H.M. Rose was unfortunately only offered in hindsight. In relation to the overall mission brief, in February 1992 the UN Security Council had authorised the deployment of UNPROFOR with the underlying suggestion that the warring parties might have to accept the continual presence of the peacekeepers, and not only in a humanitarian role. The acceptance of UNPROFOR troops within the operational area was based for the most part on consent from the warring parties, but the UN reserved the right to act in a different way if humanitarian action was threatened.

Such a 'confusion' within the mission brief was bound to lead to complexities and misunderstandings on all sides. Gradually the Command accepted other responsibilities, including peacemaking on the ground, negotiating and monitoring ceasefires, delivering aid into areas too dangerous for UNHCR, helping the refugee problem, negotiating the release of prisoners and bodies, and escorting repair missions. With this growth in new responsibilities came a demand and requirement for Civil Affairs personnel, and 'on the ground' micro-negotiation skills. But the response for the provision of such personnel, and training for other personnel, was woefully slow. A US Civil Affairs negotiator describes the role of Civil Affairs in negotiations:

> The CA team has actively taken part in most negotiations dealing with US and Macedonian locals. Negotiations with local Macedonians have centered around maneuver damage claims and land disputes. Recently with support from UNPROFOR and the Able Sentry lawyer, CA successfully resolved maneuver damage claims directed against the US. CA also participated in negotiations over landowner rights between the US Ops and Macedonian privately owned land. Involving CA early on, during negotiations over disputes between locals and US/UN military, frees the commander and leaders from this additional somewhat time-consuming burden.[3]

UNPROFOR was revealing the new operating procedures required by the serving soldier in such a situation, many of which ran contrary to established military behaviour in a war zone. These practices can be summarised as follows:

- *direct engagement*: the delivery of humanitarian supplies, rebuilding of infrastructure, 'hearts and minds' work;[4]

120

- *protection* of NGO personnel and their supplies;
- acting as *mediators* between warring factions;
- establishment of *safe* areas;
- *liaison and negotiation*: bodies, accommodation, movement.

The watching world hopes that peacekeeping missions will not merely freeze conflicts, but help to restore a sound peace as well. In a military sense this requires integration of the tactical and operational level to support the strategic aim of de-escalating violence and reconciling communities.[5] Experience in operational areas such as Cyprus shows that appropriate techniques exist at the tactical level, where peacekeepers have used arbitration, go-between mediation and conciliation to achieve ends. Principled negotiation, consultation and problem-solving meetings are thus more progressive forms of conflict-resolution, if the aim is to do more than just keep the belligerents apart physically.

COPING WITH THE NEW ROLE

The changing nature of peacekeeping inevitably brings with it new challenges. Kenneth Eyre in 1993 raised the question of training soldiers to cope with their new role:

> Given that the peacekeeping model is changing, it is fair to ask if the tasks that soldiers are now being required to do are still covered in training or general war, or if the changing face of peacekeeping now raises the imperative to train soldiers at all levels in skills that are beyond those needed to successfully prosecute combat operations. Based on experiences from the unstable environment during the Cyprus War in 1974, media reports from events in the former Yugoslavia, Cambodia, and Somalia and an informal survey conducted with several hundred troops who served in Sarajevo with the Canadian Contingent in UNPROFOR, the answer is tentatively 'yes'.[6]

The UN was forced to realise that the different roles assumed by UNPROFOR troops led to concomitant diversification in liaison and 'on the ground' duties and requirements. As the following comment implies, numerous military responsibilities required the application of negotiating techniques, which were 'critical for LOs, F Echelon leaders from patrol/ section level and up, and key CSS [Command Staff] personnel'.[7]

Although the decision to deploy was political, military commanders had to negotiate the terms on which they would support political and/or humanitarian agreements in the operational area. It is always important for the military to ensure that they are not committed to an operation which is untenable. Military units deployed to facilitate humanitarian aid had to negotiate on a case-by-case basis for freedom of movement to escort the convoys, and this often led to 'linkage' negotiations concerning other humanitarian issues and political problems that would be used as bargaining devices by and with local warlords.

Such diversity in the nature and role of military personnel in a peace-keeping situation such as UNPROFOR highlighted hitherto unknown, or unrecognised, problems for the peacekeeping soldier trying to implement UN mandates. Some of these problems even became debilitating for the force on the ground: for example, peacekeeping can involve making compromises with warring factions and therefore the impartiality of the peacekeeper is jeopardised. If consent is required in order for convoys to move and so on, it can be the case that some unsavoury deals will have to be struck on the ground. Furthermore, peacekeeping can tend to favour one side at the expense of another, again threatening the military impar-tiality factor. It is often the case that supplies are delivered to a faction whose need is greatest and safe areas established first for certain displaced peoples before others.

A soldier who is compelled to use military force to achieve an objective in a peacekeeping scenario loses his credibility for impartiality. Set-ting economic sanctions or placing pressure on a party to capitulate over a matter can appear highly partial to some of the affected parties. As UNPROFOR continued with its work such a loss of credibility made its personnel vulnerable to hostage-taking and reprisals.

In an attempt to remedy some of these dilemmas, the UN devised and distributed techniques and hints on negotiation to soldiers on the ground, reflecting upon the experiences and techniques arising from the ambigu-ous nature of UNPROFOR itself. The UN stressed that the soldier's first responsibility remained the execution of the mandate and, at every oppor-tunity, to demonstrate an unwavering resolve in the face of belligerence.[8] This might not be conducive to negotiation, however, and would go against other UN statements such as 'Negotiations are an encounter with an opponent, not an enemy. You represent the UN, and consequently have no enemy in this conflict.'[9]

It was felt that issues such as freedom of movement, neutrality and security were negotiated at the highest levels of government and in diplomatic circles, but were only effective if resolutely demanded and executed at the lowest level. Such a situation often left junior commanders with difficult choices: 'The craft of negotiation and mediation from JNCO to Coy Commander was essential, knowing how far to go before you escalate, back down or look for a new approach.'[10] Such a pressure on a young officer could be fraught with both tactical and strategic ramifications were he or she to make a poor decision.

It is rare also that a military operation embraces a paracivilian role of economic aid and assistance. However, it is more rare for the military to be involved in an economic operational commitment organised and directed by a military staff. Humanitarian relief is not such an uncommon need and is something that soldiers understand as a recognised contribution in support of civil relief operations. Most of the tasks in the field of civilian affairs have an immediate UN operational influence, and therefore the execution of these tasks is more suited to military rather than civilian personnel in a security and defence context.[11] Yet such responsibilities have important implications for the working soldier, who is trained to open fire as a response to aggression and hostility. UNPROFOR was a time for learning new lessons rapidly, reviewing 'open-fire' policy and implementing coercive resolution tactics on a daily basis. There persisted a high degree of uncertainty about how and when to use force, both at a low and high level. Some UN tasks were not covered at all by rules of engagement, for example village visitation programmes. These tasks required the blending of doctrines for convoy escort, vital point protection, and inner and outer security cordons into a single Standard Operating procedure (SOP) which then would require integration into the grander scheme of things.

Military micro-negotiation fell into this category. The perpetual and desirable dictum of negotiation/resolution of incidents at the very lowest level remained valid for most of the deployment. As participants observed:

> Negotiation was the way we always intended to achieve our aims.[12]

> I was responsible for negotiation with local police and authorities … decisions within the AOR [Area of Responsibility] were very much left to myself with minimal direction from above.[13]

Local officials tended to escalate their activities to the highest level possible, based on a premise that they need not deal with a platoon commander if a commanding officer was likely to show up. This tactic was evident in Croatia, in particular, and a great deal of persistence was shown by the soldiers to keep issues at the appropriate (low) level of command. Lieutenant-Colonel Stewart commented: '[this] is why I established a comprehensive system of liaison officers who concentrated on improving relations in a particular area'.[14]

PEACEKEEPING AND NEGOTIATION SKILLS

There was an added perceived problem for the soldiers since most of them felt inadequately trained in negotiating skills. While some had experience of working in Cyprus, many younger personnel did not, and most international units had no formal pre-deployment training package or doctrine. As we have noted in Chapter 5, many soldiers have stated that their experiences in Bosnia/Croatia indicated that you were either a good negotiator or you were not, and you had little time to alter that fact for the better. They were conscious that poorly handled negotiations could have serious ramifications beyond the immediate issue, and when cultural factors and pervading hostility were added then issues and tempers escalated in intensity. Thus a perception grew that new skills were being required of the soldiers; as well as traditional armed capability, so-called 'soft-skills' were assumed to be in their arsenal also. Shortly after the deployment of UNPROFOR, UN staff attempted to review and illustrate the new skills which had been observed on the mission.

The delineation of these factors helped to emphasise the additional skills required from the operational soldier. Here was an acceptance of two levels of tactical techniques: the normal tasks as defined on the left of Figure 8.1, and the specific peacekeeping skills as defined on the right. It was not only the UN who recognised this diversity of roles:

> In Bosnia, it was recognised that local cooperation was essential to the success of the UN expedition. For the British, this was to be very much a young captain's war ... It was these young officers, bright and some with a gift for languages, who provided the liaison officers,

FIGURE 8.1. Normal military tasks and specific peacekeeping skills.[15]

UN FORCES

PLUS

NORMAL OPERATIONAL TECHNIQUES	SPECIFIC SKILLS
OBSERVATION CHECKPOINT	NEGOTIATION
CONVOY-ESCORT PATROL	EXCHANGE OF PERSONNEL
ESCORT OF REFUGEES	MEDIA SKILLS LIAISON
SEARCH	LANGUAGE INTERPRETERS
FORCE	CULTURAL AWARENESS

to develop a 'framework of trust and confidence'. It was vital to establish working relationships with the leading civil and military personalities.[16]

In-theatre soldiers began to voice demands for training and requested that the whole area of negotiation be discussed and addressed in home-nation training packages. While the commanding officer's concept of operations and directives on the application of the UN mandate encompassed outside parameters, the substance and conduct of every micro-negotiation depended entirely on the situation in-theatre and the locals being dealt with. Soldiers who were more familiar with the country, the history, culture and conflict itself, functioned in a more confident and effective way when required to negotiate.[17] When the soldier shows a lack of appreciation of the cultural setting within which he is operating, there can be resultant problems, as one serving officer recorded:

> ... some soldiers had been sharing accommodation with Muslim soldiers. The accommodation had been dug into a hill, and during the period in question there was approximately seven foot of snow on the ground. Due to the soldiers displaying a picture of a topless woman the Muslims decided to lock them out of their accommodation. [It was resolved] ... due to the personality of one of the soldiers who had formed a relationship with one of the Muslim soldiers which helped to resolve the frosty [*sic*] situation.[18]

This was a needless predicament which had been created through ignorance of cultural standards. Resolution was achieved through the implementation of a previous relationship and trust-building stance taken by an UNPROFOR soldier, and again this emphasises the importance of the military understanding the cultural and personal context within which they are operating. However, it had been a lack of understanding that led to this incident in the first place. The problem, in one authoritative view, is a function of established military training:

> The Army's current peacekeeping training philosophy can be summed up at both the soldier and unit level as: train for war all the time and do some mission-specific training, both individually and collectively, prior to deployment. The training of soldiers, NCOs and officers at the various battle schools, leadership schools, and career courses are focused almost completely on training for war with virtually no peacekeeping specific training included ... UN-related individual and collective peacekeeping training is only conducted when a soldier, military observer [UNMO], or unit is tasked for a UN operation.[19]

The threat to convoy operations in particular was significant and to be expected throughout the operational area. UN convoys were attacked routinely by aggressors. Regional commanders of these aggressors tended to be local warlords, each with their own priorities and exclusive operational tactics, and therefore each incident had to be negotiated on a case-by-case basis. In one instance, after a local agreement was made by the peacekeepers with a particular warring faction, the opening of a different factional checkpoint was only accomplished after the arrival of the media on the scene. The belligerents did not want to appear uncooperative in front of a camera, and so they conceded the negotiation.[20]

It was readily apparent to those in the field that there was a necessity to brief personnel about the cultural setting within which they were operating, but this was not done in any formal sense in the early days under UNPROFOR. Soldiers tended to learn by experience in the field and by discussing the free flow of ideas and examples in the field, often suffering the tactical consequences if they got it wrong. As Lieutenant-Colonel Bob Stewart recorded:

> It may seem a little silly, but in Bosnia I was quickly learning that 'face' was very much about being recognised with a visit ...
>
> I had spent a lot of time with the Muslims ... in order to get across lines.
>
> We sat down at a long table ... there was a silence. I decided I had better say something ...
>
> We didn't talk much about the problems in Central Bosnia, but rather about our different backgrounds – particularly military training ...
>
> The whole incident turned a little nasty and at one stage it looked as though some British soldiers might be shot ...
>
> I asked the Muslim soldiers taking cover around the bus to direct me ... in rather a heated exchange I told what looked to be a Mujahaddin soldier that the bus and the mines were to be moved and we were to pass through. Surprisingly he obeyed me ...[21]

MICRO-NEGOTIATION

By the end of 1993 advice and guidelines on negotiation procedure were being drawn up by home nations for distribution to serving personnel, with particular reference to negotiating access, freedom of movement and humanitarian assistance scenarios. The complexity of the process was stressed, as was extensive preparation, care in execution and thorough ratification of any agreement.[22] Attempts were made to draw up rules of procedure, aimed mainly at pre-empting counter-productive techniques from the other party, described variously as 'loading the agenda', 'distortion of information', 'red herrings', 'delay', 'use of incidents' and 'non-flexibility'. A more formal view was stated as follows:

> This approach is a manifestation of UNPROFOR's resolve to protect civilian populations, regardless of ethnic background. It is not, however, UNPROFOR's intention to defend territory nor to enter the fray as a belligerent. UNPROFOR has been, is and must remain impartial. If UNPROFOR must have recourse to force, this will be in clearly defined circumstances, triggered by the actions of one or another party to the conflict.[23]

There remained an insistence, therefore, that UNPROFOR troops should seek to negotiate any resolution in a tactical situation rather than using armed force. Serving soldiers rapidly assumed such a response wherever and whenever possible, but a lack of stability on the ground meant that negotiation contexts were diverse and dangerous. UNPROFOR troops were often in physical danger, but were still expected to resolve the dilemma through cooperation rather than aggression. Here is one such case:

> The site was at an old television transmission which had been bombed by the Americans during the proposed 'lift and strike' campaign. They [the UNPROFOR soldiers] initially shared the site with a number of Serb soldiers who were guarding the communication facilities there. One night one of the Serb soldiers walked into the restroom and announced that he was going to kill himself and everyone else with the grenade he was carrying. At the time a Royal Signals Lieutenant was also present, but it was one of the soldiers who managed to calm the Serb soldier down and convince him to replace the pin in the grenade. This soldier probably succeeded in this task due to his sense of humour and the way that he managed to make friends with the Serbs before the situation arose [against orders which explicitly stated that there were to be no overtly friendly relations with any nationals].[24]

This particular situation reveals several interesting factors about military micro-negotiation. First of all there was no time for 'scene-setting' or meta-negotiation: the soldiers were pitched straight into a situation

127

which needed an instant response. If the soldiers had reacted by picking up their rifles, presuming they were to hand, the time-delay factor alone might have resulted in all their deaths. Although the killing of the Serb might be seen as a typical response by a soldier to a threat from a man armed with a grenade, it was obviously not the appropriate action in this case. A soldier, using initiative, tried to reinforce the bond he had made with the man previously; by already knowing a little about the Serb there was more information to work with and hope for a calmer resolution. He defused the situation with humour, using a lighter touch to emphasise his own calmness concerning the predicament. At no time did he 'mirror' the aggression of the Serb, instead the humour was an effective de-escalation tactic. This prior knowledge of the Serb – contrary to SOPs – was a life-saver in this situation, and emphasises the importance for the military micro-negotiator to explore the context and social norms of his operational area and its inhabitants. In this case such knowledge also gave the soldier, rather than the officer, the confidence to handle the situation. The soldier had had no previous negotiation training or experience, so his response was reactive and personal.

In many cases negotiations during the deployment of UNPROFOR began as a result of relatively minor incidents or disputes, and the nature of the incident dictated whether or not it would be treated as a crisis or as a routine conflict, disagreement or ceasefire violation. Regardless of the nature of the incident, the problem could usually be resolved through face-to-face negotiations, however protracted. Low-level tactical micro-negotiation tended to fall into two main types: *planned* and *encountered*, each having different implications for the soldier serving under UNPROFOR. Planned negotiations were used in both crisis and routine situations and were either self-initiated or requested by belligerents. Self-initiated meetings were used mainly to resolve or conduct initial introductions, the resolution of ceasefire violations, the introduction of civil affairs initiatives and military application of the UN mandate. Meetings or negotiations called by belligerents could be for similar reasons as those above, but additionally were likely to include protests against the UN, requests for humanitarian assistance or local rebuilding projects. What was stressed to personnel was the maxim that such problems should be resolved at the *lowest possible level*, thus reinforcing the demands made at a junior level for successful micro-negotiation. As some post-operational reports from Canada argue:

> Negotiations normally begin as a result of an incident or sit [situation]. The nature of the incident will dictate whether or not it will be treated as a crisis or as a routine conflict, disagreement or

ceasefire violation. Regardless of the nature of the incident, the problem will normally be resolved through face-to-face negotiations. For reasons of simplicity, two types of negotiations have been ident [identified]: planned and encounters.

Planned negotiations are generally formal structured meetings between belligerent, UN and/or civic representatives and are usually conducted at the HQ or sub-unit level. They may be used in both crisis and routine sits depending on the complexity of the problem, the urgency of the sit, and the personalities involved.

Encounter negotiations are spur-of-the-moment negotiations entered into by a mil [military] member to resolve minor incidents or sits. The Golden Rule is to negotiate and resolve problems at the lowest possible level, before they can evolve into bigger issues.[25]

An unplanned encounter which turns into further planned negotiations, with the pressure of resolution at the lowest level, can be also be seen in the description of the incident which follows. This serves to exemplify many of the unique aspects of military micro-negotiation discussed already:

The journey went without incident until we were stopped at an HVO checkpoint ...

'Please get out of the car so we can search it.'

His action was familiar and predictable, so I shoved under his nose our newly acquired guarantee of respect for our status and safety, signed by his commander-in-chief, the general in charge of all HVO forces in Bosnia-Herzegovina ... When he had read the official document, he nonchalantly tossed it onto the floor of the car with a contemptuous snort and informed us that in these parts, he was in charge ...

'Search or stay where you are.'

We tried to show him the letter again – this time he disdained even reading it. We were left with no alternative but to turn back ...

The next morning ... straight to HVO Military Police HQ to be given an explanation for the remarkable incident of the previous day. To make sure there were no misunderstandings, we took our interpreter with us ... The duty officer ... had never seen or heard of this document and could not care less. All he wanted to talk about was gun-running for the Armija BiH. Discussion was obviously fruitless and I changed tack and explained the purpose and practicalities of our mission and the importance of our neutrality. It seemed to do the trick – this was information he could handle and before long he had promised to call the checkpoint in question and give orders for our free passage.

... what we had just witnessed was evidence of a total lack of military discipline ... [people were] outlaw warriors – people fighting their own personal vendettas in blissful independence of the agreements reached by the superiors who were running the war.

The military personnel were then shelled the next day by the HVO.

We called the SMO over the radio and asked him seriously to consider another shut-down of our observation post because as far as relations between the Croats and the UNMOs were concerned, we had reached a state of constant confrontation.

Our Croatian liaison officer advised us ... there were indeed HVO units that were less than delighted with our presence and which operated outside the military chain of command.[26]

Many of the elements of military negotiation analysed and defined within this book are present in this scenario:

- sense of power in own area
- ignoring outside directives
- predictable disruption
- military sense of predestined failure of negotiation, but persistence is attempted
- one group not knowing what the other is doing
- use of an interpreter
- interpreter knowledge of contextual situation and feelings
- military stressing impartiality
- total confrontation resulting in UN job becoming untenable
- frustration.

Unfortunately only some of these factors were delineated in the current training and information packages, with the UN emphasising factors such as impartiality to its personnel, and with less stress on the influence and effect of cultural awareness, or the lack of it.

The issue of 'not losing face' is emphasised in the interpersonal interaction in negotiation, but in military operations it plays an important part in the maintenance of personal credibility and integrity within oneself, and as an overt message to one's own 'troops'. Command depends on a high degree of authority and confidence in any given situation, and a tactical negotiation is no different from a firefight in that sense. The idea of maintaining a psychological 'advantage' over the other party is very appealing in tense situations, such as those experienced in military tactical operations.

In an incident of a different kind,

> A Company of 1PPCLI was involved in negotiating an incident which lasted 11 hours, ending at 0200hrs. The entire negotiation took place at a road intersection in the Zone of Separation [ZOS] with the hood of an Iltis being used as the negotiation table. Be prepared to negotiate by day or night, in all types of weather. Be able to sustain your negotiating team with hot beverages and food. This will sustain the alertness and endurance of the negotiating team and have a strong psychological effect on the person with whom you're dealing.[27]

Not every negotiation in theatre was a roadblock-type scenario. As the above account shows situations were diverse and therefore testing to the personnel trying to achieve a resolution. Pre-theatre training tended to concentrate on roadblock negotiation alone, and it was not until several deployments had passed that pre-theatre negotiation training encompassed other scenarios as well.[28]

Many post-exercise reports stressed the need for training to include negotiation instruction in all pre-deployment briefings for *all* units, whatever the nationality.[29] Psyops (psychological operations) units were formally briefed in such procedures anyway, and it was felt that such information was a valuable source for wider application of negotiation technique to a greater number of interested parties.[30] The Psyops emphasis on obtaining the latest intelligence on all participants, interests and issues prior to negotiating with them was felt to be pertinent and sensible.

For the UN, military negotiation and mediation on Peace Support Operations (PSO) had the ultimate aim of reaching agreements to which all parties had consented freely and which would help to contain or de-escalate the conflict, and this remains the accepted view to this day.[31] As a PSO created objective and effective negotiation situations, controlled and fostered at every level, so it was hoped that a climate of mutual respect and cooperation would develop from such an approach. Increasing importance was placed on the commander at the scene, with the need to evaluate, identify and address the sources of the incident to find the best level of response.

INCREASED OFFICIAL GUIDANCE

Gradually, guidance on how to handle peacekeeping negotiations began to appear in training manuals and operational directives. Captain J.M. Faure, in a UN directive, wrote:

> In all conflict situations, the Force should try to achieve a return to peace through re-establishing dialogue between the parties. The members of the Force, each of them according to their various levels of function and position, should actively attempt to convince the parties to negotiate. Force members must position themselves to listen and understand, so as to be able to suggest mediation and compromise. Continuous dialogue with the parties in conflict is essential to the success of a peace-keeping mission.[32]

From these sort of statements one can detect the emphasis on key strategies for the military negotiator to employ in the operational area; for instance, there is repeated use of terminology such as 'impartiality', 'control', 'use of force' and 'credibility'. Another training directive stressed the protracted nature of negotiation:

> As with all UN missions the conduct of negotiations with opposing forces, incl civs, is crucial to the success and implementation of new programmes and the resolution of longstanding problems. Negotiations at even the lowest levels tend to be protracted affairs which reqr extreme patience and perseverance. Negotiations are also complicated by the fact that both sides have a complex chain of comd with an extensive bureaucracy. Comds at all levels can expect to conduct negotiations with representatives from all levels of gov incl: mil forces, civ pol, local municipal auths, and even influential civs.[33]

As the realisation of the importance of negotiation techniques grew within the operational area, then so too did the acknowledgement of its place within peacekeeping skills *per se*. Figure 8.2 delineates the place of negotiation in PSOs, and demonstrates its function and relevance in peacekeeping skills.[34]

Figure 8.2 stresses the context within which peacekeepers operate, both on the situational and operational levels of a mission. It illustrates the dilemma facing the peacekeeping force when 'sandwiched' between warring parties, and the 'pull and push' effect of external agencies and influences upon those serving in the field. With strictures and demands

FIGURE 8.2. The principles of action within a peacekeeping operation.

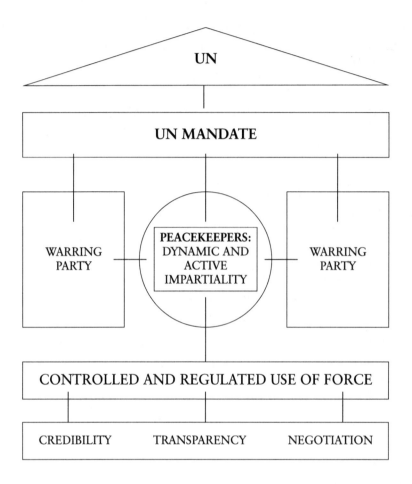

such as those illustrated above, it is not surprising that, without a high degree of awareness of the mutability of the mission, any of the influential factors might affect the standing and action of a tactical group at any time within that mission. The peacekeepers are having to 'look' several ways when engaged in such a mission: to guidance from the UN mandate, the operational and the tactical judgement of the applicability of the use of force (which itself is a result of an assessment concerning negotiation as the first form of dispute resolution), and to the nature and context of the warring parties involved.[35] It may be suggested that within Faure's inner circle of peacekeepers there ought to be a further distinction between multinational personnel with differing ROEs and SOPs, thus causing another complication in the tactical decision-making process.

CONCLUSION

UNPROFOR, with all its inherent difficulties, was a useful learning experience for military personnel in the sense that the multiplicity of roles and tasks placed upon the modern peacekeeper were highlighted together with a perception that they should not be overlooked or assumed in any way. Many post-operation reports from a diversity of nations stress the omnipresent negotiation encounter in the field, and its complexity.[36] Many also surmised that, of all the skills required in the preparation and conduct of productive peacekeeping operations, negotiation was one of the most important but least-practised duties in the pre-deployment phase. It was deemed important because, through compromise and the exchange of ideas within theatre, relationships could be formed to permit a tenable agreement to maintain the peace or the truce. However, negotiation is among the least-practised skills because it is still regarded by some as a skill not associated with, or included in, day-to-day military training. Fortunately, this is a view which is diminishing as peacekeeping operations repeatedly show the strength and validity of negotiating in theatre, and that it is a requirement at all stages of an operation, and at all operational levels from the inception of a mission to its termination.

It is easy with hindsight to denounce and deprecate the role of UNPROFOR, but to do so is to overlook the contention that it was on this mission that the UN was forced to face head-on the realities of peacekeeping in the late twentieth century. Whilst this meant that the role for personnel on the ground could be confusing and limited at times with little room for manœuvre, it also revealed the evolving nature of the peacekeeping soldier and the personal demands such work was making on the individual. Therefore it allowed, and is still allowing, the review and amendment of both deployment and pre-deployment preparedness.

NOTES

1. Information taken from an open source issued by the Army Lessons Learned Centre, Canada, written on a CD dated November 1997, version 5.0.
2. H.M. Rose, 'A Year in Bosnia: What was Achieved', *Studies in Conflict and Terrorism*, 19: 221-8 (1996), p. 223.
3. US document cited in Army Lessons Learned Centre, Canada, CD ROM November 1995.
4. A term devised by Templar.
5. Compare the proceedings under UNPROFOR with specific guidance given in Operation RESTORE HOPE (Rwanda): 'In humanitarian operations ... [all] must be intimately involved in what the other is doing, and must make an extra effort to ensure that the other is appraised of every activity, meeting,

encounter, and operation conducted by the other.' Post-operation report (non-attributable).

6. Dr Kenneth Eyre, comment at symposium on 'The Changing face of Peace-keeping', Canadian Institute of Strategic Studies, 1993.

7. 12eRBC Mid Tour Report, CANBAT 2 Roto 2, cited on website *http://www. allc.com/website/english/products/dispatch/3-1/dis313ae.htnl*. LO is an abbreviation for liaison officer.

8. Ref. 77/4 B-77/4, Annex B, SOP 2/5/1 05231996.

9. Ibid.

10. Non-attributable comment, Operation Grapple soldier.

11. I understand (from a non-attributable source) that in the summer of 1998 discussions took place amongst NGOs as to whether an armed Red Cross would be more effective than the present organisation. Such an organisation would bridge the two areas of responsibility. However, it was felt to be inappropriate.

12. Lieutenant-Colonel Stewart, *Broken Lives* (London: HarperCollins, 1993), p. 317.

13. Non-attributable comment from an Operation Grapple soldier.

14. Lieutenant-Colonel Stewart, *Broken Lives*, p. 317.

15. My adaptation and enlargement of a figure in Captain J.-M. Faure, *Commanding United Nations Peace-keeping Operations: Methods and Techniques for Peace-keeping on the Ground* (New York: UNITAR–POCI, 1996), p. 87.

16. C. Bellamy, *Knights in White Armour* (London: Random House, 1997).

17. Summary of non-attributable comments from former UNPROFOR personnel.

18. Non-attributable account given to author.

19. Non-attributable, Canadian Forces Command and Staff College, Toronto, March 1994.

20. Example cited in A. Morrison, D.A. Fraser and J.D. Kiras (eds), *Peacekeeping with Muscle: The Use of Force in International Conflict Resolution* (Toronto: Canadian Peacekeeping Press, 1997).

21. Excerpts from Lieutenant-Colonel Stewart, *Broken Lives*.

22. Non-attributable account related to the author.

23. Report of the Secretary-General Pursuant to Resolution 844 (1993), S/1994/555, 9 May 1994.

24. Non-attributable account from a British officer to author.

25. Document 05231996 OPS0047E, Army Lessons Learned Centre, Canada, CD ROM November 1995.

26. S.B. Husim, *At War Without Weapons* (North Branch, MN: Airlife, 1998).

27. 1 PPCLI Op Harmony Roto 4, POR report cited on the website *http://www. allc.com/website/english/products/dispatch/3-1/dis313ae.html*.

28. I refer to the excellent pre-theatre training which takes place at the FIBUA village on Salisbury Plain, UK. Currently many national armies send their troops to be trained in peacekeeping skills, which include negotiation, prior to deployment. Themes include negotiating for accommodation and negotiating the removal of illegal checkpoints, for example.

29. Conclusions drawn from non-attributable material which cannot be quoted here due to classification settings.

30. Psychological operations.

31. Detailed reference is made in this section to Lieutenant-Colonel P. Wilkinson

and Lieutenant-Colonel R. Rinaldo, *Principles for the Conduct of Peace Support Operations* (New York: UN Institute for Training and Research, Programme of Correspondence in Peacekeeping Operations (UNITAR–POCI), 1996).

32. Statement from Captain J.-M. Faure, *Commanding United Nations Peace-keeping Operations*, p. 71.
33. Document 05231996 OPS0047E, Army Lessons Learned Centre, CD ROM November 1995.
34. Captain J.-M. Faure, *Commanding United Nations Peace-keeping Operations*, p. 71.
35. In the case of Bosnia, of course, there were three warring parties, which further complicated the interaction on the ground.
36. Where classification allows, examples of such comments have been cited in this chapter.

9

Mediation in Moldova: A Case of Second-track Diplomacy

KEITH WEBB

INTRODUCTION

In recent years a great deal has been written and published on the subject of mediation, ranging from Alternative Dispute Resolution (ADR) in domestic or neighbourhood disputes, mediation in communal conflicts, to international mediation. It is now fair to say that there is a communicable literature – a subject – in existence which would not have been so true 20 years ago.[1] The reasons for this are not hard to find. The revolution in communications have made all parts of the globe part of the discourse of humanity, if not equally so. The 'CNN effect' stimulates governments everywhere. Increasing interdependence has meant that events in one country spill over and affect others – an effect which is enhanced by almost universal participation in the liberal economic market-place. Further, particularly since the end of the Cold War overlay, norms of intervention have been shifting and human rights have become more strongly articulated.

At the same time the nature of conflict has been changing. Whereas the classical literature on organised violence concentrated on war between states, the contemporary concern is much more to do with civil wars. Between 1990 and 1995 over five million people died through organised violence, not to mention the millions of internally and externally displaced refugees.[2] In wars at the beginning of the century, over 80 per cent of casualties were combatants, in contemporary war over 80 per cent of casualties are civilians.[3] The situation is exacerbated by the presence of ever cheaper weapons. The favoured weapon of killing is not the smart or brilliant weapons of the advanced industrial countries, but the automatic rifle, of which up to 72 million have been manufactured from the end of the Second World War to 1990.[4] The machete is also popular.

Two further features of contemporary conflicts may be noted. The first is that they are, in the main, regionally concentrated. Some areas of the world are virtually conflict-free, while others seem constantly riven.[5] Secondly, while identity has always been an important feature of human existence, in the modern world it forms an important element of many conflicts. Traditional factors, such as economic competition and territory are, of course, still important, but are often articulated in terms of identity.[6]

The consequence of these trends has been the recognition of a problem. How is the international community to deal with the plethora of conflicts in the world? It is impossible to envisage a world policeman with the will or the capability to suppress these conflicts. The United States, unwilling to cross the 'Mogadishu line', is reluctant to assume the role, and the UN, while putting an increasing number of peacekeeping forces into the field and organising sanctions in others, is incapable through resource scarcity of managing world conflicts. One answer to these problems is the increased use of mediation.

Mediation, compared with other forms of intervention, is relatively cheap. It takes persistence and some skill, and if done properly does not usually make the situation worse even if it does not always bring about the desired result. It is an activity that can be undertaken by a wide variety of actors, from states, to international organisations, to individuals, and in different circumstances each may have unique contributions to make.

THE CENTRE FOR CONFLICT ANALYSIS

The Centre for Conflict Analysis (CCA) was started in 1964 by John Burton, a former head of the Australian diplomatic service. It was, and is, a loose collection of scholars from a number of countries who are interested in the causes and resolution of conflict. Burton and the first generation of members of the centre (for example, Light, Banks, Groom, Mitchell, de Reuck, Oppenheim, etc.),[7] propounded what was then a novel view of the world, known colloquially as the 'world society' model. At that time at the height of the Cold War and in the aftermath of the Cuban missile crisis, realism and the idea of power politics was the dominant view of the way in which international politics operated. Burton *et al.*, with some prescience, envisaged the world as a 'cobweb' of relationships in which the state was only one, albeit important, actor on the world stage. In a sense they were the vanguard of pluralistic views of international society, anticipating globalisation long before the nature of these trends fully emerged. As part of their general theory the unit of analysis was moved from the state (or the international system) to the individual (or the relationship). Further, in seeking the *causes* of conflict it was held to be rooted in the frustration of human needs such as security, participation, identity, etc. While many of the things that people desire were believed to be of a zero-sum nature, this was denied by the World Society school. It is not the case that if I have more security, you have less; or if I have more identity then you have less. Sometimes the obverse is true in that the more I seek to ensure my security with the purchase of arms, the end result is increased insecurity as opposing parties do likewise.[8] Having re-evaluated the nature of international society and conflict, the next step was to devise some means of conflict-resolution. The answer came in two parts: the development of the idea of second-track diplomacy and the formulation of the problem-solving workshop.

SECOND-TRACK DIPLOMACY

A distinction is often made in the literature between 'first-track' and 'second-track' mediation or diplomacy. The former is a formal process conducted by high-status actors such as other states, the UN or OSCE (Organisation for Security and Cooperation in Europe). The latter is a low-profile approach often conducted by actors with little formal political status, for example, the Sant' Egidio Community in Italy which was so successful in the Mozambique settlement.[9] The distinction, while valid, is often in practice blurred with high-status actors intervening informally and out of the glare of publicity. Magwiru indeed refers to this as 'third-track' diplomacy, and identifies it as a peculiarly African mode of inter-vention.[10] Further, it is not unusual for first- and second-track actors to interact. For example, Pickvance in the South Tyrol dispute interacted with both the Italian and Austrian negotiators.[11]

There are a number of major problems with first-track diplomacy. The first is the problem of recognition, particularly in communal and civil disputes. In many conflicts the 'legitimate' party will not recognise publicly the other party. Hence for many years the British government refused to talk to the Irish nationalists, branding the IRA (Irish Republican Army) as criminals. To 'recognise' them would give them legitimacy and credibility. To label them as 'criminals' and 'terrorists' rather than 'free-dom-fighters', enabled the government to treat them in a particular way, and through this definition attempt to deny them alliances. In the end, of course, except in the case of total victory, there has to be talk. So Kenyatta,

Mugabe, Mandela and Adams had to be treated as *interlocuteur valables* on the path to settlement. Often, however, the public redefinition of status has to be preceded by low-key contacts where there is no open acknowledgement. Thus, as early as 1984, members of the National Party in South Africa were attempting to set up a meeting with the ANC (African National Congress), and the British government had unacknowledged contact with the IRA for years before the Northern Irish peace process became public. Second-track actors can perform a low-key linkage and meeting function where the 'legitimate' party can communicate with the dissident party without having to acknowledge them publicly. Talk has to happen eventually, unless there is a total (and unusual) victory for one side, and second-track actors are often better placed to facilitate this than first-track actors.

A second reason for a low-key approach is the problem of constituency pressures. High-profile third-party intervention conducted in the glare of publicity gives leaders little opportunity to be flexible. Only rarely are parties wholly homogeneous with respect to the peacemaking process, and leaders in public forums need to look over their shoulder and not to appear weak. Thus in the recent Kosovo conflict, Albright, Holbrooke and Cook (at Rambouillet and before) announced what they were going to say to Milosevic *before* meeting him. What this did was to drive Milosevic *and themselves* into a corner from which neither could retreat without loss of face. Most peace processes end in a first-track agreement, but the ground needs to be carefully prepared beforehand. In moving towards peace new positions have to be taken, and this is often difficult because of leaders being 'entrapped' by their former positions.[12] Further, it is often felt that the lives and cost sacrificed in the conflict would be betrayed by talking to the opposition and thinking of peace rather than victory. It is sometimes the case that new leaders will emerge unencumbered by the baggage of the old leadership, as with de Klerk, Gorbachev or Rabin. Even so, political opinion will have to be forged and public opinion is prepared for the change over time. In this process second-track activity can be of crucial importance.

Thirdly, to be seen to be talking to the enemy is sometimes seen as an act of treachery or betrayal. Thus Mengistu had 12 of his generals shot for talking to the EPLF (Eritrean People's Liberation Front) when Eritrea was fighting for independence from Ethiopia. The perception of betrayal occurs for two reasons. To engage in violent conflict can be a moral act of a high order. There are people who enjoy killing and/or the excitement of war, but in the main before engaging in, for example killing a neighbour (as in Rwanda, Bosnia or Kosovo), some deeply felt justification is needed. Changing or compromising one's beliefs is not like changing a shirt; it is often a long and painful process and is nearly always accompanied by internal dissent within the parties.

All third-party mediators bring resources to their efforts. Thus, at Camp David, the United States was able to broker a deal partly due to the economic and military resources it could supply to the disputants. The resources supplied by CCA and other similar organisations, paradoxically flows from the fact that politically they have no status. There is no threat involved, nobody is made to do anything and all participants are there of their own free will. The only resource is skill and knowledge. What CCA does is to exploit the peculiar status of the academic. In almost every society men and women of 'knowledge' or 'wisdom' have respect, and in a mediatory situation this can be exploited. People will often talk to an academic in a way that they would not to others.

THE PROBLEM-SOLVING WORKSHOP

The theory and practice of the problem-solving workshop (PSW) as an aid to conflict-resolution was developed by Burton, Azar, Kelman and the other CAA theoreticians cited on p. 138.[13] Rather than looking at and analysing conflict from the outside, Burton and his fellow academics believed, first, that the academy should be involved in the world rather than merely observing and, second, that by being involved in a practical manner they would learn more about how conflicts could be resolved.

Early theories of the PSW stressed human needs. This emphasis stemmed from Burton's analysis of the causes of conflict, which were located in the frustration of human needs.[14] According to this perspective, the purpose of the PSW was to uncover the needs of the conflicting parties and, since they are variable, to discover means through which they could be met. Later approaches to the PSW have been more humanistic, driven to redress the a-cultural nature of human needs theory. Väyrynen, for example, drawing on Schutz, sees the PSW as creating a common 'space' within which parties can live and understand each other.[15]

Within the PSW community there has been much discussion about the *level* at which intervention takes place. Some have argued that ideally workshop activity should start at the bottom, aiming to influence and educate future decision-makers.[16] In time there would be a spread of alternative perspectives in the society which would lead to greater acceptance of settlement agreements. If this is possible it would ease the 're-entry problem' (see below), but it is only rarely practical. Setting up a PSW can take months of communicating with the participants, often involving many visits to the location in question. It is also expensive, and fund-raising is often far from easy. 'If there were but world enough and time ...' – but there never is! The tendency, therefore, is to aim for a level which would have some fairly immediate political impact. Typically, this would be just *below* the top political leadership. The leaders themselves would carry too much baggage, be too high-profile, and discussion would too soon turn into negotiation or a barren restatement of positions. However, the delegates that do attend the PSW need both to be approved by the major political leadership and to have the ear of that leadership.

Typically a PSW will take place a long way from the site of the conflict. The reason for this is that it effectively isolates the participants from their day-to-day routine. There are no secretaries, colleagues, telephones, faxes, etc. to distract the participants. For several days they have nothing to do or think about apart from the conflict and how to resolve it. In such circumstances the possibility of new and creative thinking is enhanced.

The question arises as to why the leaderships of conflicting parties should agree to take part in a PSW? First, they would normally see themselves as being in an intractable situation. The parties themselves cannot see any way out; the conflict is costing dearly, but neither side can win or lose. Often there is an element of crisis – high anxiety, lack of palatable options and pressures of time. Sometimes this situation is described as a 'hurting stalemate' – but hurting stalemates can go on for many years. In the case of Moldova, from being one of the more prosperous autonomous republics within the USSR, after independence and the civil war, it is now one of the poorest regions in Europe, on a par with Albania. So the situation emerges where the parties are looking for a way out, but are often constrained by the problems of entrapment, recognition and constituencies noted previously.

But why *this* third party? In general, in any conflict, there are more third parties willing to mediate than can be used.[17] It is often the case that a particular third party is acceptable to one party but not the other, and vice versa. For second-track diplomacy of the kind noted here, three factors are important. First, reputation and past record. An organisation such as CCA or FIS (Foundation for International Security) is more likely to be accepted if there is proven experience and a record of success – or, at least, a record of no disasters. Secondly, such an organisation is often legitimised by others. Thus the CCA intervention was encouraged by the OSCE and indirectly supported by the FCO (Foreign and Commonwealth Office). Thirdly, it has to be an 'appropriate' intervention. During the long night of the Northern Irish troubles, an organisation similar to CCA attempted second-track diplomacy between the contending parties and was given 24 hours by the nationalists to get out of the province. The intervenors were mostly English and seen as inherently biased by one side!

We have already touched on the problem of 're-entry'. During the five or six days duration of a PSW (particularly if the exercise is a continuing process), the delegates may develop understandings and interpretations that are not shared by the rest of their respective parties. Hence, when they 're-enter' their own communities difficulties may occur *vis-à-vis* communication. While it is one of the aims of the PSW to develop novel ways of resolving the conflict, these have to be communicable. For this reason it is useful to have at least some persons in each delegation who are known 'hawks' or 'hardliners'. Their 'conversion', should this occur, will normally carry more weight than that of known 'doves'.

A related problem is that of continuity. No conflict, to my knowledge, has ever been resolved in one meeting. Normally conflict-resolution is a long drawn-out affair, necessitating many meetings and involving a multiplicity of actors. Two steps forward and three back are not unusual. The reasons for this are not difficult to see. Such situations are always marked by great distrust, and confidence-building takes time. Further, there is usually a great sense of hostility and hatred, and finally there are the internal politics of each party. For the third party it can be a frustrating experience, as third parties often do not take part in the day-to-day prosecution or management of the conflict, and this means that things may have moved on when a subsequent workshop occurs. This is so even when there is on-site monitoring between workshops. To some extent this can be managed by asking the delegates to update the third party, which is useful for the purposes of exploration (see below), but errors of inter-pretation are easily made. A further continuity problem can occur with the introduction of new personnel in the delegations. This can happen, for example, by a change in the political hierarchies of one or both parties. On the one hand it may be argued that this expands the area of influence in that more people are undergoing the process, but, on the other hand, it often means 're-educating' new people to the nature of the process.

It should be noted that a PSW is not a forum for negotiation. Negoti-ation *per se* is seen as primarily a first-track activity. In the Moldova case, as in many others, there is a blend of first-track and second-track, with organisations such as CCA, MICOM (Moldova Initiative Committee of Management), IA (International Alert), FIS and others working in one way but in complementary fashion to the third-party activity of Russia, the Ukraine and the OSCE. Rather the PSW is designed to *explore* the conflict as a problem to be solved. The delegates are invited to a PSW, which, it is stressed, is an academic exercise where the delegates help the academics understand the conflict. Typically, one 'side' would be asked to explain what the conflict is about to the panel. (This may take an entire day!) At certain points the panel may require clarification. During this process the other side is requested not to intervene, although disagreement will often be seen in the shaking of heads, snorts and sometimes even incredulous laughter. Then the other side gives their version of events, again with occasional interventions from the panel. Sometimes the whole process is slowed down through the need to use an interpreter. In the first Moldovan workshop, one side insisted on speaking Romanian and the other Russian, while most of the panel spoke English. This was a sensitive matter since language was one of the early issues in the conflict. In subsequent workshops only Russian and English were used.

The important point to note here is that while one side is communcating with the panel, they are also communicating their perspectives to the other side, and vice versa. It is often believed that conflict occurs through a lack of communication. Personally, I believe this to be rare. In most of the conflicts I know about there have been real issues at stake where parties' perceived vital interests are threatened. But one of the consequences of violent conflict – of all kinds – is an immediate diminution of communication. What happens then is that each party begins to interpret the behaviour of the other. In a situation of high distrust and hostility, for security reasons a worst-case analysis is often used, where the intentions of the other party are seen as being far more extreme than in fact they often are. The consequence of this is that each party sees itself as being rational and reasonable, while the other party is irrational and unreasonable to the point of being positively evil. Hence, stereotyping and simplified perceptions emerge as a *consequence* of the conflict rather than being the *cause* of it. Take the following example: the leaderships of two parties meet for a conference hosted by a third party. Certain undertakings are given. A leader goes back and gives a speech to his faithful followers in which he reiterates pre-conference rhetoric. The other side becomes aware of this and sees it a gross act of bad faith. In fact, of course, the leader giving the speech has a constituency that has certain expectations and cannot make big leaps. He is responding to his perceived political necessities, but this is *interpreted* as duplicitous behaviour.

What will often happen is that the party going second will use the occasion not only to put their point of view but also to rebut the interpretations of the side going first. Thus a response must be allowed. In all dealings with the parties extreme impartiality must be observed. Thus, if in one session one party begins, care must be taken that in the next session the other party starts things off. Parties are *always* suspicious and looking for bias and partiality. (In one case one party went to check on the hotel the other party were being housed in to make sure that they were getting equal treatment!) Depending on the case in point, it is sometimes easier to sympathise with one party rather than another; for instance, in the

South African case it is difficult for a liberal humanitarian British academic not to be anti-apartheid. But *treating* parties impartially is a professional skill needed by the third party. If either of the parties come to believe that the third party is in some sense not impartial, the usefulness of the workshop is close to being at an end.[18]

There are two further aspects of the 'process' that are particularly useful to the facilitator. The first is the introduction of a comparative perspective into the PSW. It is usually the case that people engaged in a particular conflict will consider *their* conflict to be unique, even to the extent of believing that an outsider cannot understand it. In one sense of course they are correct, but in another they are clearly wrong. Each conflict is a peculiar constellation of factors and personalities never before encountered in history, and no outsider is going to understand it in the same way as a participant. I, as an outsider, will never understand in the same way that an Afrikaner, an Irish nationalist, or a Kosovan Albanian will understand their conflicts. However, as well as being unique, every conflict has generic features, and it is to these that the facilitating panel will draw attention. The facilitating panel, who should be knowledgeable about a number of conflicts, will begin to make comparisons with respect to the causes, conduct and settlement of other conflicts. This activity serves a number of purposes. It provides *information* to the participants and allows them to see new options and alternatives. Thus, with respect to the Moldovan conflict, rather than just talking about other conflicts, both delegations were taken to Northern Ireland and participated in the analysis of that conflict. On another occasion the facilitation team pulled in constitutional experts to explain the principles and varieties of constitutions. The experts were then questioned by the delegates. A further function performed by the comparative activity is that it draws the delegates into an *analytic* mode of thought. If all goes well, they cease to think about those 'bastards' on the other side of the table and rather begin to explore their common problem in a spirit of cooperation. It is also my belief that engaging in comparative analysis helps with the re-entry problem. Individuals can go back to their communities with information and knowledge that allows them to speak with greater authority and increases the probability that they will be listened to.

A second activity the facilitation team will engage in is a *costing* exercise. While a conflict will often provide benefits for those engaged in it, such as status and prestige or feelings of solidarity, there are also usually severe costs to violent conflict. It is usually fairly easy, at least in ball-park figures, to count the dead and maimed, but there are other less obvious costs to conflict. Sometimes the dead are seen as martyrs, and to talk peace a betrayal of their sacrifice. But most conflicts do come to an end eventually, and the future possibilities have to be weighed against the past cost and the present actuality. Less obvious costs are the traumas in the society suffered by those who have suffered, are maimed, or who have lost loved ones. What has happened in the past can happen in the future if some sort of settlement is not achieved. There are also development costs. Waging war, or even preparing for it, is an expensive business, and it is usually education, health, individual and societal wealth and culture that suffers. The facilitation team will attempt to draw out those costs and make them explicit, and in so doing lay out the vision of a better future once the conflict is settled.

Thus the PSW is attempting to change the perceptions of the participants. This is not 'manipulation' or 'social engineering'. None of the delegates will change their minds or open themselves to new ideas unless they want to. Neither is the facilitation team undertaking these activities without the knowledge of the participants. They are told what the team is doing and why they are doing it. Since the facilitation team typically has no power, the delegates are free to leave whenever they want to, but in my experience they have always gone along with the process and stayed to the end.

THE MOLDOVAN CASE

One of the problems in developing the theory and practice of the PSW is the sparsity of case-histories. This is understandable due to the confidential nature of the exercise. Much more case-study material has been written on formal first-track mediation than informal second-track facilitation and mediation. Hence this section will note the process and dynamics of CCA's involvement, but is unable to discuss in any depth the dialogue and deliberations that took place in particular workshops.

The Moldovan conflict is in some ways more open to resolution than many conflicts. First, it was a 'new' conflict in that there was no long heritage of past conflicts between Moldova and Transdnestra[19] shaping the perceptions of the actors. It would thus not fall into the 'protracted conflict' category noted by Azar.[20] Second, it is primarily a political conflict as opposed to ethnic or religious, even though language and irredentist tendencies were among the early issues. The importance of this is that it becomes possible to 'fragment' the conflict, that is, it is possible for the parties to trade and bargain. This is much more difficult where the primary issues involve religion or ethnicity: how does one go about fragmenting religion or identity? Third, even in the early aftermath of the civil war, both parties appeared to recognise that they had a common

146

destiny and that in some fashion they had to live together. Thus, in terms of resolution cases, the Moldovan conflict is very much at the easier end of the spectrum. Even so, the involvement of CCA has lasted nearly eight years.

'Moldova' as an autonomous Soviet socialist republic was a consequence of the carve-up of Eastern Europe as a consequence of the Molotov–Ribbentrop Pact of August 1939, the territorial loser in this case being Romania. The territory known as 'Transdnestra' was tacked on to the Moldovan territory, the wider region being previously known as 'Bessarabia'. The dominant language of Moldova was a dialect of Romanian (now called 'Moldovan') while in Transdnestra the dominant language became Russian, due to the influx of large numbers of workers to man the industries of Transdnestra. Hence, with the collapse of the Soviet Union, the attempt by the Moldovan government to change both the script and the official language of the country was strongly resisted. In addition, there was initially a strong party (a faction whose strength has since declined greatly) which wanted reunion with Romania, which was again resisted. Added to this were issues related to the location and relocation of industrial plant. Transdnestra was the industrial base of what was largely an agricultural economy, and the central government wanted to broaden geographically the industrial base. A further element concerned the nature of governance and economy: Transdnestra wishing to remain closer to the former USSR model, the Moldovans wishing to move to a market economy, closer to Europe than to the CIS. The Transdnestrans declared independence – a move that eventually led to a civil war, after which they were able to maintain their *de facto* independence and statehood. But they were not recognised by the international community, and Moldova remained the state with *de jure* recognition. The civil war in 1992 was short but nasty. Accurate figures as to the number of casualties are hard to come by. The fighting was ended by the Russian 14th Army, commanded by General Lebed, intervening and freezing the situation. The presence of the Russian army has become a major source of complaint for the Moldovans, while the Transdnestrans see it as a security guarantee.

The involvement of the CCA occurred through a circuitous route. Following the war, a Northern Irishman, Joe Camplisson, was running community development projects in an attempt to build functional relations between the erstwhile combatants. Relations between the two governments were so bad that little or no progress was being made. Camplisson realised that in order for development to occur, and for cooperation between the parties, there would first have to be a resolution of the conflict. In pursuance of this end he contacted CCA and proposed a PSW.

While there have been numerous other first- and second-track interventions, CCA has been involved in three PSWs held at the University of Kent at Canterbury: one in Belfast hosted by MICOM, two at Adderbury hosted by FIS, a constitutional conference in Kiev in March 2000, and several post-conflict reconstruction seminars. In between these meetings (which spanned a seven-year period) numerous visits have been made to Moldova and Transdnestra to monitor agreements, observe developments, talk to other third parties and arrange further meetings.

During this period the whole nature of the interaction between the parties has changed a great deal. The first PSW was marked by intense hostility – it was held not long after the killing had stopped. The parties would not travel on the same airplane, or in the same bus, or use the same language (even though both parties were fluent in Moldovan and Russian). Over the years this has changed, but progress has been painfully slow and often talks have been deadlocked. Some of the tension went out of the situation when changes were made in the nature of border patrols, and when a non-use of violence agreement was signed, brokered by the Ukraine, Russia and the OSCE. Often in meetings the delegations would just keep repeating positions, sometimes not even bothering to change the words. Thus unusual measures were needed in order to keep the momentum and to break a log-jam. On one such occasion each participant was asked to write on a piece of paper three things the other side could do to help them, and three things they could do to help the other side. This generated some 72 propositions which the facilitating team condensed down into nine 'principles', which formed the agenda for the following two days and were the basis of a post-workshop report to the two presidents. Sometimes, due to political expediency, it was necessary to move away from the pure form of the second-track PSW. At one of the Canterbury workshops the participants requested that there should be ambassadorial representation from Russia, the Ukraine and the OSCE,[21] which changed the whole nature of the process. It is worth noting that while there is good 'theory' about how a PSW should be run, rarely is it possible to conduct a workshop in a formulaic manner.

CONCLUSION

The second-track intervention in the Moldovan–Transdnestra conflict has been slow, at times confusing, often frustrating, but ultimately *successful*. Transdnestra and Moldova are now playing the end-game, and edging towards a constitutional settlement which will probably be guaranteed by the three first-track mediators. There was a constitutional conference in

March 2000 in Kiev, where constitutional lawyers from six countries laid out the bones of a possible constitution. This is still being discussed, and it will probably take another two years before a final settlement is reached.

How then can the second-track contribution made by CCA over the past seven years be evaluated? My belief is that the 'Kentski' process has made a valuable contribution on the path to settlement, but it is impossible to estimate the precise value of that contribution in isolation from the myriad of indigenous interactions and first- and second-track external inputs. Perhaps in the long-run such an evaluation does not matter; what does matter is that violence has ceased, a settlement is close and, as a result of that, greater economic prosperity is on the horizon.

NOTES

1. Much of this literature deals, however, with principles and practices. There is something of a dearth of detailed case-studies, as noted later, largely for reasons of confidentiality. See M. Light, 'Problem-Solving Workshops: The Role of Scholarship in Conflict-Resolution', in M. Banks (ed.), *Conflict in World Society* (Brighton: Harvester/Wheatsheaf, 1984,), pp. 146–60.
2. D. Smith (ed.), *The State of War and Peace Atlas* (Harmondsworth: Penguin, 1997), pp. 26–7.
3. M. Kaldor, *New and Old Wars* (Cambridge: Polity Press, 1999), p. 8.
4. 'Tackling the Problem of Light Weapons: The "Micro-Disarmament" Policy Debate', *Light Weapons*, 4: 2 (March 1998), pp. 1–2 (abstracted in *Small Arms and Light Weapons: An Annotated Bibliography, Update 1996–1998* (Canada: Department of Foreign Affairs and International Trade, 1998), pp. 58–9).
5. Smith (ed.), *The State of War*, pp. 90–5.
6. J.A. Vasquez, *The War Puzzle* (Cambridge: Cambridge University Press, 1993), pp. 123–52.
7. See M. Banks (ed.), *Conflict in World Society*.
8. See Vasquez, *The War Puzzle*, p. 180.
9. See, for example, *http://www.santegidio.org/en/contatto/cosa_e_txt.html*.
10. M. Magwiru, 'The International Management of Internal Conflict in Africa: The Uganda Mediation, 1985', PhD thesis, University of Kent, 1994.
11. T.J. Pickvance, 'Third-Part Mediation in National Minority Disputes: Some Lessons from the South Tyrol Problem', in C.R. Mitchell and K. Webb (eds), *New Approaches to International Mediation* (New York: Greenwood Press, 1988), pp. 131–46.
12. F. Edmead, *Analysis and Prediction in International Mediation* (New York: UN Institute for Training and Research, 1971).
13. See Banks (ed.), *Conflict in World Society*.
14. J.W. Burton, *Dear Survivors ...* (London: Pinter, 1984), *passim*; J.W. Burton, *Global Conflict* (Brighton: Harvester/Wheatsheaf, 1982), pp. 139–40; J.W. Burton (ed.), *Conflict: Human Needs Theory* (Basingstoke: Macmillan, 1990).
15. T.H. Väyrynen, 'Sharing Reality: An Insight from Phenomenology to John

Burton's Problem-solving Conflict-Resolution Theory', PhD thesis, University of Kent, 1995.

16. C. Mitchell and M. Banks, *Handbook of Conflict Resolution: The Analytical Problem-solving Approach* (London: Pinter, 1996).

17. K. Webb, 'The Contingency Model of Mediation in the Yugoslavian Conflict', in J. Berkovitch (ed.), *Resolving International Conflicts: Theory and Practice of International Mediation* (Boulder, CO: Lynne Reinner, 1996).

18. For information on the organisation and management of PSWs see Mitchell and Banks, *Handbook of Conflict Resolution*.

19. People spell 'Transdnestra' in different ways. Here the simplest spelling is adopted.

20. E.E. Azar, *The Management of Protracted Social Conflict* (Aldershot: Dartmouth, 1990).

21. These are referred to by the parties as 'the mediators'. They have been active throughout the process and have made many important contributions. The activity undertaken by CCA has been referred to by the parties as the 'Kentski process'.

10

Why Russians React as they Do: How Culture and History Influence Behaviour and Responses during Negotiation

ALEXANDER KENNAWAY

No wise intelligence officer should ask himself 'what would I do if I were in someone else's shoes?' The essential issue is to understand what are the driving forces that impel him to act, think and react the way he does.[1]

Individuals tend to band together to form tribes whose leaders formulate or even invent a history and a set of myths which they mould into a common subconscious. This may be done at tribal meetings, in schools and through other formal and informal ways, passing from parent to child. This set of assumptions and beliefs is based on what is accepted as facts, often carefully selected to foster a particular spirit amongst the people which suits the leadership. Down the ages there are further accretions of selected assertions which enter the folklore. In this way the group identity and love of country are fostered. This may have harmless and indeed beneficial results, but often the reverse occurs. This chapter seeks to analyse the extent to which a national character can affect international communication or cooperation.

In discussing these elements with respect to Russia, I am not suggesting that each by itself sets Russia apart from other nations. But it is the composition and the proportions of the mix that identifies a nation or indeed, as some would say, a civilisation. Some people ask if Russia is a unique civilisation or a set of nations and countries – a question which has been debated and fought over in Russia between the Slavophiles and the Westernisers. Some, including Peter the Great, wanted to modernise, and in so doing assumed that Russia had also to Westernise. If that meant adopting a democratic rather than an autocratic regime, the rule of law to protect the individual rather than the state, then we can see at once the gap between the two concepts. To some degree Russia has modernised, but only to a far lesser degree has it become Westernised. Personally I do not accept the assertion that Russia is a unique civilisation.

Extreme nationalism is an engine of psychological and mental imbalance. In some countries – Germany and Russia spring to mind – nationalism is probably the engine that creates other, subsidiary myths which disturb the psychological state and well-being of their leaders and people. This affects them not only in the obvious manifestations such as military and political aggression but in other important ways. Extreme nationalism invents and exaggerates fundamental differences from other groups, with whom one may even be coexisting in a small region. This perception of difference may smoulder for decades until a trigger is provided which causes it to burst into unreasoning and lethal hostility. To take a contemporary example, this is the case in Former Yugoslavia.

The myth of one nation of pure Slavs has led Russia to go to war twice to support its 'Slav' brothers in Serbia, and recently we saw the threats by Yeltsin and Lukashenko against NATO in Kosovo to form the Slav triad. Similar traits can be found, to a lesser degree perhaps, in almost every other country in Western Europe, the United States and Japan. This suggests that the basis upon which we might consider ourselves to be superior (and there-fore to be able to teach the Russians) is severely constrained. Such advances as we have gained have taken decades, indeed centuries, to evolve. Even if the Russians were 100 per cent convinced that they had to adopt Western ways there is no reason why they should be able to do so more quickly than we have. So, while we consider the specific Russian attributes, let us bear in mind the second assumption and avoid any temptation to flaunt an assump-tion of superiority of our culture against theirs. History shows, further-more, that people, especially with such a history as theirs, are somewhat touchy if they think they are being treated as inferiors, especially when they and their country are plainly going through a difficult transitional period. To ignore Russia and its interests and attitudes in such circumstances is a recipe for an international confrontation which is totally unnecessary.

THE SHOCK OF THE LOSS OF EMPIRE

The Russian empire is a land empire contiguous with its heartland, Muscovy, and of its dominant people. At various times during the past the Russian empire expanded in every direction from Muscovy. Russian losses following the withdrawal from its Warsaw Pact allies in the late

1980s were followed by the disintegration of the USSR in 1991; the CIS cannot be regarded (except by certain Russians) as the new Russian empire. Russian expansion into the empire began hundreds of years ago, and Russians as farmers, workers, administrators, soldiers, retired pensioners (together with those exiled and deported by the authorities) have lived in these territories for centuries. Except for the deported nations, they regard their place of abode as 'home'. Indeed, most of them have no other home and no means of acquiring one back in Muscovy. Like other colonisers, the Russians have had their ups and downs in their relations with the 'colonised', but in their own mind the Russians have been the superior people and imposed their own culture on the 'natives'. For these reasons the Baltic republics, the Ukraine, Belarus, the Caucasus and the areas of central and eastern Siberia are 'ours'. Under the Soviets the separate republics were only independent on paper – and who in the Soviet Union ever paid any attention to paper, especially constitutions? The republics were fully integrated into every aspect of the Soviet system. Their economies were interlinked with those of the territories dependent upon the needs, orders and supplies of materials and components largely from Russia. Indeed, the whole military system created by the Soviets was interlinked. The Soviet officer corps was almost entirely composed of Slavs, with Russians predominating, followed by Ukrainians and Belarussians. The Ukraine occupies a special place in Russian history, heart and mind. It was the origin of Christianity in Russia, and of the Russian Orthodox religion, language and alphabet. In spite of the usual battles between neighbouring lords, the relationship from the Russian point of view has been one of harmony and indeed identity of culture. Naturally, Ukrainian nationalists who struggled for independence from Turk, Pole, Hungarian, Swede and Russian alike, saw it differently. But the separation of the Ukraine into an independent state is more of an affront to Russians than the separation of other republics.

The withdrawal from the garrisons of its Warsaw Pact allies and from the Baltic republics and Ukraine has had two devastating effects on the Russian armed forces. The first is the retreat into the homeland of hundreds of thousands of officers who regarded their garrisons and barracks as their permanent homes; they, like the civilians in the empire, had no other. Many retired locally in congenial areas such as the Baltic republics. Other favoured locations were to be found in the south, in 'our' territories of the Caucasus and the Crimea. In the good old days the Soviet army could provide retired officers with a flat or a dacha there or in the capital cities of their choice. The retreat coincided with the collapse of the Soviet economy, which provided the main reason for the political and military chaos following the events of August 1991. (Of course, the collapse of the economy was itself due to the over-militarisation of the Soviet Union and to the incompetence and inefficiency of its centrally directed command economy, but that is a subject for a different book.)

The second catastrophic effect, from the point of view of the Russian Ministry of Defence, was the loss of all the forward bases, garrisons, early warning systems, repair workshops, depots and living quarters. All these have had to be relocated within Russia itself. The means for doing so were limited, although ameliorated by the German government paying for their location, training and building of accommodation for the garrisons stationed in the DDR. Furthermore, the MOD was slow in planning for the moves; some divisions were dumped into open fields and left to improvise their living and other quarters. As a result many officers were justifiably disgruntled, unhappy with their lot and their government and politicians. Small wonder that there are many in the armed forces who see the withdrawal (and its architect, Gorbachev) as having betrayed their loyalty. The Russian armed forces continue to see their need to prepare to engage in future conflict as a massive, high technology force and that their potential opponent continues to lie in the West.

Military thinking delegates the containment of unrest within the Russian Federation to the troops belonging to one or other of the 17 ministries with armed or paramilitary forces. They continue to think so apparently even after the poor performance of the internal troops in Chechnya.

THE RUSSIAN LANDS

The vast spaces of the Russian lands affect Russians in much the same way as Americans are affected by the vastness of their country, with their romantic and perhaps distorted historical view of the Wild Frontier.

The Russian lands were sparsely populated, with widely separated settlements, so mutual support was paramount for survival in a hostile climatic environment with a very short active agricultural season, even in the areas of rich farm land. This is not conducive to rugged individualism. So collectivism is a natural way of life, rather than private ownership of land and private farmers. It was not invented by the Bolsheviks, but they perverted it.

Collectivism existed in pre-Christian Russian society, followed by the *mir*, the *obshchina* and *artel*, in which the peasants were accustomed to settling their own working conditions, even as serfs whose lives were controlled arbitrarily by their owners who were agriculturally more ignorant and incompetent than the serfs. A peasant society is inherently

154

conservative; old ways die hard. The practical effects of serfdom, abolished in part by law in 1861, lasted certainly until 1905. Consequently Russian agriculture was inefficient, with a huge rural proportion of the total population. It was not accustomed to creating the large surpluses needed to feed the urban population that grew apace after the First World War. This was a basic reason for the famines, later made much more severe by the dogmatism of the Bolsheviks.

Even today we are looking at primarily a far-flung and extensive rural society – 25 per cent of the population are rural workers (compared with 1.5 per cent in the UK). As recently as 1939 the figure was over 60 per cent. When you are a hundred miles or so out of the big cities, you are back a hundred years in the conditions of life. Long winters render rural populations inactive; there is little for the uneducated amongst them to do but drink their own fermented and distilled alcohols. Alcoholism is, not surprisingly, a major element of all illness in Russia; despite education it becomes an acceptable habit.

Not surprisingly the instincts and attitudes of a peasant society go deep even in an urban industrialised and militarised society. Incidentally, the Russian armed forces, just as they did in tsarist times, still own, run and man very large farms. They have not dared to rely on civilian farming, not even the much vaunted collective farms, to feed themselves. Most city-dwellers still have their own allotments and rely on them for much of their food.

THE RUSSIAN VIEW OF THEIR ROLE IN EASTERN AND CENTRAL EUROPE

Winston Churchill brought into the open in his speech at Fulton in 1948 the views of many in the West that Stalin's Russia was bent on occupying Western Europe by force of arms. In Churchill's view the move away from independence and democracy promised by Stalin at Yalta for these countries, coupled with the maintenance of large garrisons, were signs of aggressive intent. But most Russians regard his expansion into Europe as the establishment of a safe buffer-zone against perceived Western potential aggression. The speech stimulated especially the fanatical anti-communists who had also been pro-fascist in the 1930s; it also made possible the careers of people like Senator McCarthy who discovered a streak of gold in anti-communism. There are other possible conclusions. Firstly that the Soviets were determined to create a *cordon sanitaire* in Eastern Europe to prevent yet another attack to follow the many that historically had come from that direction. This view follows the traditional suspicion of foreigners discussed later in this chapter. It is also reinforced by geography: western Russia, with its flat plains, has no natural defensive features. In these circumstances extra space, especially someone else's, provides a breathing space and a battleground preferable to one on Russian soil. History provides reasons for the defensiveness and suspicion of foreigners of the Russians.

From the east came the Mongols – under leaders such as Ghenghis Khan – who subdued the Russians for several hundred years from the thirteenth to the early eighteenth century. The Russians derived much of their autocratic, arbitrary habits and system of government from the Tartars (as they became known). But towards the end of their rule the Tartars intermarried with their former subjects, each contributing to the leading groups of the other. In their turn the Russians slowly expanded north and east into the largely empty spaces of Siberia, reaching the Bering Straits in the fifteenth and sixteenth centuries. The Crimean Tartars were the most formidable. Thence, the Tartar nomads had also expanded over much of Europe and the southern countries on both sides of the Mediterranean intermingling with Turkish and Iranian tribes, Greeks and other myriad tribes of Asia Minor. All of these were pretty warlike, creating and losing empires over the centuries. These usually contested with the Russians the same territories which we now know as the Caucasus, Crimea, Ukraine and the Baltic states. These contests brought about the formation of armed settlers and farmers in the south. These were formed partly from the armies of the rulers – local Slav kings and tsars of Russia – and partly from deserters and renegade subjects of the petty kingdoms. The latter became known as Cossacks, who are not – as they would like to pretend – an ethnic entity. They ultimately entered the service of the Tsars, but throughout history Cossacks also took part in peasant revolts against the nobility. From the west and northwest, Muscovite and Kievan Russia also suffered many invasions from various combinations of Poles, Swedes and Lithuanians who in the Middle Ages formed powerful kingdoms and alliances. Russians regarded Poles not only as hostile aggressive peoples but also, since they had embraced Catholicism, as enemies of Orthodox Christianity. The Russian Tsarist dynasty concentrated its power under the slogans 'Autocracy', 'Church' and 'Nation'. The Russian Orthodox Church has been more noted for its support of rulers, however tyrannical, than for liberal opposition to them – even in the Bolshevik era. Even today the hierarchy finds good reason to do nothing about ecumenical relations with other Christian churches, especially the Roman Catholics and Greek Catholics (otherwise the Uniates) now active once more in Belarus and Ukraine.

Russians still find it easy to assert that they are surrounded by enemies, and this gives credence to the assumption that Russia needs a large armed force. The domination of many lands and peoples during the Tsarist empire and under the Soviet Union reinforces the assertion that Russia is a great power which must command respect. For respect one may read 'fear'. It was a Greek who said of the Roman Empire, 'let them hate us provided they fear us'. That Russia today can no longer prevent the United States from its own military adventures is a source of shame to nationalists and also fuels the demand for a visibly powerful armed force. It even provides an argument for its nuclear deterrent, 'without which Russia would be powerless'. At the same time Russian strategists assert that nuclear weapons are unusable in today's world. The illogicality of this position defies argument.

Historically the Russian state has rarely launched an aggressive war. In 1890 it had designs on Korea, fomented by the ultra-nationalist Admiral Alexeyev. In 1939 the attack on Finland can be seen as a defensive, pre-emptive strike against a regime sympathetic to Germany with a border merely a few kilometres from Leningrad. Red Army training exercises after the Second World War usually predicated a NATO strike which had to be repelled by a massive counter-blow. It is probable that plans to invade Western Europe, to occupy the Rhine and the channel ports, featured more in Western than Russian imaginations. Perhaps the most dangerous period was under Khrushchev, whose macho ideas were stifled in the 1962 Cuban missile crisis. It is almost certain that during the Cold War the military on both sides used their arguments of potential threats from the other side to increase support for military expenditure. The Russian people have never exhibited the latent, and sometimes patent, chauvinism and support for expansion that has for example characterised the German nation.

Most Russians today view themselves as a defensive people; they can be mobilised for defence of the homeland but do not support adventurism, not even in Chechnya. (Many a regimental commander had conscripts dragged out of barracks by their mothers. However, the lies and deceits of the authorities concerning the Afghan war helped to turn the old patriotism of many Russian women to hostility to military service for their menfolk.)

One has also to reflect upon the experiences of West European powers in their own retreat from empire. The British withdrawal fortunately coincided with the upturn in demand following the end of the Second World War; the economic conditions, although not altogether favourable, were better than those which have faced Russia. It was possible for British servicemen and civilians alike to return 'home', to find a home and pay their way whether in retirement or in a second career. The French have had a less pleasant experience in their withdrawal, especially from Algeria. This was both legally and emotionally regarded as part of metropolitan France: the colonisers regarded it as their permanent home. France, even today, has a large immigrant population of both 'native' French and Algerians, many of whom do not feel integrated into French life and do not wish to be French. This is exploited by the fascist, nationalist French political Right. French experience is not unique; other countries, including Germany, Portugal, Belgium and Holland – and even Greece and Turkey – have not been free of difficulties with and hostility towards foreign ethnic immigrants and minorities. The experience should provide grounds for at least sympathetic understanding of the Russian predicament.

PATRIMONIALISM

This term has been used to describe the Russian state under Tsarism, but it still applies today. Briefly, the Tsar, or the current regime in power, assumes that the country and its resources belong to them and can be used as they wish.

The fundamental laws of the Russian empire defined the Tsar as 'unlimited' and 'autocratic'. This meant that he was subject neither to constitutional nor institutional constraints. He was the exclusive source of laws. Tsar Nicholas II, completing his return in the first national census in 1897, gave his rank as 'first nobleman of Russia' and his occupation as 'Master of the Russian land', while his German wife described herself as 'Mistress of the Russian land'. His reactionary concepts led Russia to defeat in 1914–17, to social ruin and to the subsequent victory of the Communist Party. It was he who ruled by the slogan 'Faith, Loyalty and Autocracy'. His 'ministers' were powerless; they had to wait upon his pleasure, as did the Duma (the Russian parliament). It is true that he, like Alexander II, felt impelled to give a little to sharing power with the aristocracy and the educated classes. However, these occasional relaxations in autocratic power were followed by further repressions as the fear of democracy getting out of hand was reinforced by events.

The general secretaries of the Communist Party, Lenin and Stalin, were also all-powerful; their associates lived in fear and had little influence on the policies. Their successors retained much of that power, although it was to a greater degree shared by the Central Committee. This resulted in the enforced retirement of Khrushchev. Brezhnev managed to avoid being forced out. A forceful, intelligent (but ailing) Andropov would almost certainly have re-established central power and authority had he lived. Yeltsin, an old Communist Party boss, tried to follow the line in his relations with his 'government'. It was the only way he knew. His own 'cabinet' promulgated *ukazes*. The decision to go to war in Chechnya was almost certainly taken within his Security Council without time being given to the Ministry of Defence to lay the proper planning, training and logistic support for the armed forces. It gave every impression of a sudden 'whim', a caprice, to use the Russian term. At the same time his ministers treated their ministries as personal fiefdoms to provide opportunities for the enrichment of themselves and their friends. There was no coherent cabinet or governmental policy; ministers fought each other for their own 'line' and privileges. Honest ministers tended to resign. However, Yeltsin had to take some notice of the Duma, although he played off one faction against another. He made conflicting statements to them and to Western governments.

The political history of the Western world from the fifteenth century to the dawn of the twenty-first has seen a general increase in democracy, perhaps punctuated by some reversals from time to time in some countries. In Russia, by contrast, the rule of autocracy over the same period has been at best constant, and for long periods became more rigid with time, although some modest and shortlived relaxations have been visible. This is the unfortunate inheritance of the rulers and peoples of every part of the former Soviet Union. By no acceptable definition is contemporary Russia a democracy. It would be a miracle if it were to move steadily towards a democratic society. Russia has no experience of:

a) accountable and delegated responsibility;
b) political parties with coherent programmes – with the exception of the Communist Party;
c) the rule of law to which the state itself is also subject. The Russian experience is one of arbitrary law without justice. Where the law is applied it is used to maintain order, rather than to ensure justice.

SUSPICION OF FOREIGNERS AND FOREIGN IDEAS

Suspicion of foreigners has always been prevalent in Russia. In olden times Russians were forbidden to travel abroad without permission of the Tsar; if they did so their families could be tortured, executed and have their property confiscated. Foreigners could enter only with special permission, and their places of abode and itineraries were restricted. Contact with foreigners was discouraged, and until 1703 all domestic and foreign news was considered to be a state secret. Especially important was the preservation of the true religion against ungodly Europe. Every aspect of nationalist and religious propaganda is pressed into service even today. The KGB has released some papers to show that the Catholic Church was conniving with Western military plans to invade Russia with the aim of supplanting Orthodoxy. The KGB penetrated the Orthodox hierarchy before and during the Second World War, and has unashamedly exploited its appeal to the people. The Decembrist rising in 1825 was organised by young nobles who had been in France after the defeat of Napoleon and absorbed some revolutionary democratic ideas. As a result, Tsar Nicholas I increased political repression, forming the 3rd Section of the Imperial Chancery, which acted as an intelligence body penetrating every 'subversive' organisation. Stalin almost automatically exiled or jailed large numbers of Soviet people, even ex-POWs who had lived under German occupation during the Second World War because of the 'contamination' that they might have received.

Currently Russians are preoccupied with the following suspicions and grievances:

- Western engineers trying to help to improve the competitiveness of the Russian military–industrial complex now have all the defence secrets and thus obviate the need to have intelligence agents in Russia. Pratt & Whitney offered to spend $20 million to modernise a firm making aero-engines and to acquire a modest stake in the share equity. The management refused, on the grounds that the Americans would thereby acquire and exploit their cherished secret advanced military technology. Pratt & Whitney's vice-president stated that they had found nothing worth having in design or manufacturing technology – indeed it was all so obsolete that similar ideas had been withdrawn in the United States a decade or two previously.

- By admitting foreign world-class firms, needed to improve the performance of the mineral extraction, transport and manufacturing, Russians are selling their birthright to foreigners.

- Norwegian researchers into ecological damage in the Barents Sea are spying on the military.

- By allowing a Western firm to re-record old performances by top Russian musicians, the country is selling its national treasures. (The contract provided for royalties to be paid to Russian artists.)

This phobia derives mainly from the fact that from the tenth century onward, Russia has been attacked and invaded by Tartars, Turks, Poles, Swedes, the French (under Napoleon), French and English in the Crimean War, Germans in the First and Second World Wars, the Japanese in 1905, the English and their allies during 1919–21, as well as Afghans and Muslims. Since 1917 the hostility has been compounded by 'class enemies bent on destroying the first Socialist State'. Events from 1945–91 are seen through Russian eyes as continuing the ring of enemies bent on the destruction of the Soviet Union.

The following extract typifies the sentiments of even quite balanced Russians:

> We are a proud people with over a thousand years of civilised history. Every intervention from foreigners has been to the detriment of Russia. We saved Western civilisation from tyranny at least three times: once from the Tartars whose occupation we endured for 300 years; once from Napoleon; and more recently from Hitler. We have learned in the past how to absorb and adapt foreign ways to suit our circumstances. No one can save us except ourselves. If you do not like our way of doing things or our policies and you threaten to remove your aid in order to make us follow your wishes then we will do without your aid. Our ability to survive, to suffer, to endure hardships for decades, indeed centuries, is legendary and we will do it again rather than bow the knee to suit foreigners.

This is the 'heroic' view of Russian history, and Westerners should bear in mind that it is one that is held by many Russians today.

ECONOMIC PROBLEMS: MATERIAL DEPRIVATION

The poor quality of goods and equipment is evident today in every walk of Russian life. Even excellent fundamental research by military scientists is degenerated at the industrial phase because of poor quality equipment and materials. Some Russian weaponry is brilliantly conceived, but its engineering is often feeble and degrades the original idea. This is not surprising when one examines the military factories, many of which are badly laid out, with equipment that varies from the unacceptable (i.e. obsolete) to the best imports poorly operated and managed so that the reject rates are acceptable only in a society that neither knows the cost of manufacture nor cares about waste of resources.

Today Russia still imports technology and tries to pay for it by exporting raw materials. It has done so for the whole of this century. Russian industry is apparently incapable of producing cost-effective basic things: for example, the machines needed urgently to consolidate railway tracks (these were always imported but now there is no money for them). Consequently, the railways suffer more derailments and delays. (The road-making equipment used to spruce up the main roads into Moscow for the 850th celebrations was all Italian.)

Russia also imports one-third to half its food, plus unnecessary consumer goods and luxuries. This trade enriches some individuals whose pockets would be hit if Russia embarked on a sensible policy of import substitution. That would be quite a job, however, since the designers would have to learn from foreign firms and there would need to be a revolution in management as well as in the industrial system itself. But these truths are not accepted by the majority in the leadership, since Russians are brought up to believe their own mythology and tend not to challenge it.

THE EFFECTS OF MARXISM

Marxism, or more accurately the Leninist–Stalinist version as an obligatory straight-jacket for thinking, is a sort of procrustean bed for graduates of Bolshevik academies. It created a significant number of pseudo-intellectuals who dominated the Communist Party and state. It crippled the habits of thought of many still in high places today, not only in Russia but also in Central and Eastern Europe. Of course the brightest, as in any country, survived even this system of education. It is noteworthy that many of the top people in the old KGB are amongst the most intelligent and cultivated people in the former Soviet Union, probably because they did not believe the rubbish they disseminated among the people. This is in contrast to the 'partocrats' – people from humble origins, brought up and educated within the party schools rather than at a proper university.

RUSSIAN DISILLUSIONMENT WITH THE WEST

After its brief and unsuccessful flirtation with the West, there is some evidence that Russia is now attributing its present state to evil Western policies. NATO is again being cast as the enemy. A report by the Institute for Defence Studies (supposedly commissioned by the Defence Ministry) concludes that 'the US and its allies represent the main threat to Russian national security', and recommends a return to a nuclear stand-off and reoccupation of the Baltic states to counter Western attempts to isolate and destroy Russia (*Segodnya*, 20 October 1995). The institute also recommends economic protectionism, a military-nuclear alliance with

Iraq, Iran and Libya, and the creation of a new state including Russia, Belarus, Kazakhstan and the Ukraine. Duma Defence Committee Chairman Sergei Yushenkov, a member of 'Russia's Choice', said the report is a cause for concern as it reflects the mindset of at least some of the Russian high command.

WESTERN APPROACHES TO RUSSIA

The following are some examples of some Western attitudes which are at best counterproductive and at worst extremely unhelpful:

'Communism is dead, capitalism won.' This is a frequently heard comment, especially from Americans. We might ask which version of Western capitalism we are talking about. Are they all successful in delivering well-being to the nation? And is communism really dead? Did it not provide for the mass of the people in the Soviet Union and elsewhere in Eastern Europe a better life than they are experiencing now? And is this not why practically every country in Central and Eastern Europe has returned communists in one guise or another to power? The Russians see that whereas in Western Europe we have, to varying degrees, a civilised form of capitalism, with in the main, effective legal means to bring to justice those who perpetrate economic crimes, theirs is a 'capitalism of legalised robbers', many of whom are in power.

'Russia must acquire a parliamentary democracy: without it membership of the EU and NATO will not be possible.' This has been the chorus of advice from the West. How long did it take us, Great Britain for example, to evolve a true parliamentary democracy with full and equal adult suffrage? How long has it taken for governments to consider the wishes of the people, to pass laws that would be obeyed and therefore could be policed? The Royal Navy has a phrase 'Different ships, different long splices'. In other words, there is more than one way of going about a job; one has to understand it, respect the reasons for it before attempting to alter it. Western-style democracy cannot simply be grafted onto a country with a culture (and I define culture in its widest sense of 'the way of life') so different to that of the West – a fact that Western politicians would do well to remember.

CONCLUSIONS

In summary, those involved with Russian nationals in situations of negotiation or mediation should bear in mind the following points:

- Russia is still driven by its old, inherited forces.
- The resources of the state belong to whatever regime is in power.
- The heads of government fight for power, privilege and spoils.
- The state is not subject to legal constraint.
- There is an assumption that centrist direction and policies are the only way for Russia.
- There is a prevailing spirit of suspicion and distrust of everything foreign, accompanied by an extreme sense of defensiveness rather than expansionist aggression.
- Extreme nationalism glorifying Russianness is very easily fostered.
- The loss of empire after the break-up of the Soviet Union in 1991 has resulted in a catastrophic decline in living, health and environmental standards, law and order, the social fabric, increased crime and blatant corruption.
- Nationalists, communists and their various allies have all exploited Russia's identity crisis and are happy to lay the blame at the door of the West and of the Russian reformers.

All the above are exacerbated by Western attitudes of superiority, by disdain of even the most modest appeals to take Russian sensibilities into account, for example, in NATO. In the tumultuous events of Eastern Europe the cultural inheritance of the Russians needs to be considered, if we wish to cooperate and negotiate with them. As we have seen, theirs is a culture profoundly different to that of the West, and we cannot afford to forget that fact if we wish to make progress.

NOTE

1. I am indebted to my colleague Lieutenant-Colonel Dr A. Clayton, Intelligence Corps (retired), for drawing my attention to this remark by Brigadier Williams, who was Montgomery's chief intelligence officer.

Bibliography

Aldis, A. and Dick, C., *Central and Eastern Europe: Problems and Prospects* (London: HMSO, 1998).

Allen, C., *The Savage Wars of Peace: Soldiers' Voices 1945–1989* (London: Michael Joseph, 1990).

Allen, T., *War Games: Inside the Secret World of the Men who Play at World War III* (London: Heinemann, 1987).

Avruch, K., *Culture and Conflict* (New York: Institute of Peace Press, 1998).

Bacharach, S. and Lawler, E., *Bargaining: Power, Tactics and Outcomes* (San Francisco, CA: Jossey-Bass, 1981).

Barston, R.P., *Modern Diplomacy* (Harlow: Addison Wesley Longman, 1997).

Bartos, O.J., *Process and Outcome of Negotiations* (New York: Columbia University Press, 1974).

Bazerman, M., 'Negotiator Rationality and Negotiation Cognition', in H.P. Young (ed.), *Negotiation Analysis* (New York: John Wiley, 1988).

Bercovitch, J. and Rubin, J.Z., *Mediation in International Relations: Multiple Approaches to Conflict Management* (Basingstoke: Macmillan, 1992).

Berdal, M.R., 'Whither UN Peacekeeping?', Adelphi Paper no. 81 (London: International Institute of Strategic Studies, 1993).

Berridge, G.R., *Talking to the Enemy: How States without 'Diplomatic Relations' Communicate* (Basingstoke: Macmillan, 1994).

Bienen, H.S., *Armed Forces, Conflict, and Change in Africa* (Boulder, CO: Westview Press, 1989).

Bierman, W. and Vadset, M., *UN Peacekeeping in Trouble: Lessons Learned from the Former Yugoslavia* (Reading, MA: Ashgate, 1999).

Blechman (ed.), *Force without War* (Washington, DC: Brookings Institute, 1978).

Boutros-Ghali, B., *An Agenda for Peace: Preventive Diplomacy, Peace-making and Peace-Keeping*, Report of the Secretary-General Pursuant to the Statement Adopted by the Summit Meeting of the Security Council on 31 January 1992 (New York: United Nations, 1992).

——, *Supplement to an Agenda for Peace*, Position Paper of the Secretary-General on the Occasion of the Fiftieth Anniversary of the United Nations (New York: United Nations, 3 January 1995).

Bramley, P., *Evaluating Training* (London: Cromwell Press, 1996).

Brotherton, C., *Social Psychology and Management: Issues for a Changing Society* (Milton Keynes: Open University Press, 1999).

Brown, R., *Social Psychology: The Second Edition* (New York: Free Press, 1986).

Burk, J. (ed.), *The Military in New Times: Adapting Armed Forces to a Turbulent World* (Boulder, CO: Westview Press, 1994).

Burt, G. (ed.), *Alternative Defence Policy* (New York and London: Croom Helm, 1988).

Burton, J.W., *Conflict and Communication* (New York and London: Macmillan, 1969).

——, 'The History of International Conflict Resolution', in E.E. Azar and J.W. Burton, *International Conflict Resolution: Theory and Practice* (Brighton: Harvester/Wheatsheaf, 1986).

Caplan, R., *Post-Mortem on UNPROFOR* (London: Brasseys, 1996).

Carnall, G., *To Keep the Peace: The United Nations Military Force* (Chicago, IL: University of Chicago Press, 1976).

Charters, D.A. (ed.), *Peacekeeping and the Challenge of Civil Conflict Resolution*, proceedings of the sixth annual Conflict Studies Conference (Fredericton, New Brunswick: University of New Brunswick, 1994).

Chomsky, N., *The New Military Humanism: Lessons from Kosovo* (London: Pluto Press, 1999).

Cimbala, S.J., *Coercive Military Strategy* (College Station, TX: Texas A & M University Press, 1998).

Clarke, M., *Simulations: In the Study of International Relations* (London: Hesketh, 1978).

Coakley, T.P., *C3I: Issues of Command and Control* (Washington, DC: National Defense University Press, 1991).

Coates, J., *Women, Men and Language* (Harlow: Longman, 1993).

——, *The Ethics of War* (Manchester: Manchester University Press, 1997).

Cohen, R., *Theatre of Power: The Art of Diplomatic Signalling* (Harlow: Longman, 1987).

Connaughton, R.M., *Swords and Ploughshares: Coalition Operations, the Nature of Future Conflict and the United Nations* (London: HMSO, 1993).

Connor, W., 'Nation-building or Nation-destroying', in *World Politics*, 24 (1972).

Connors, B., *Mission Possible: Making United Nations Peace Operations more Effective* (Newport: US Naval War College, 17 June 1994).

Corwin, P., *Dubious Mandate: A Memoir of the UN in Bosnia, summer 1995* (Gloucester, MA: Duke University Press, 1999).

Coulon, J., *Soldiers of Diplomacy: The United Nations, Peacekeeping, and the New World Order* (Toronto: University of Toronto Press, 1998).

Cronin, P.M. (ed.), *From Globalism to Regionalism: New Perspectives on US Foreign and Defense Policies* (Washington, DC: National Defense University Press, 1993).

Daniel, D.C.F. and Hayes, B.C. (eds), *Beyond Traditional Peacekeeping* (New York: St Martin's Press, 1995).

Davis, L.E., *Peacekeeping and Peacemaking after the Cold War* (Santa Monica, CA: Rand, 1993).

de Bono, E., *Conflicts: A Better Way to Resolve Them* (Harmondsworth: Penguin, 1991).

Dennehy, E.J. (ed.), 'A Blue Helmet Combat Force', National Security Program Policy Analysis Paper 93-01 (Cambridge, MA: Harvard University, John F. Kennedy School of Government, 1993).

Deutsch, M., *The Resolution of Conflict* (New Haven, CT: Yale University Press, 1973).

——, *The Resolution of Conflict* (New Haven, CT: Yale University Press, 1977).

Diamond, L., *Beyond Win/Win: The Heroic Journey of Conflict Transformation* (Washington, DC: Institute for Multitrack Diplomacy, 1996).

Diehl, P., *International Peacekeeping* (Baltimore, MD: John Hopkins University Press, 1994).

Dougherty and Pfaltzgraff, *Contending Theories of International Relations* (Harlow: Addison Wesley Longman, 1996).

Douglas, A., *Industrial Peacemaking* (New York: Columbia University Press, 1962).

Druckman, D., *Boundary Role Conflict: Negotiation as Dual Responsiveness* (paper presented at International Studies Association, St Louis, March 1977).

Dunn, D.H. (ed.), *Diplomacy at the Highest Level* (Basingstoke: Macmillan, 1996).

Durch, W.J., *The United Nations and Collective Security in the 21st Century* (Basingstoke: Macmillan, 1993).

—— (ed.), *The Evolution of UN Peacekeeping: Case Studies and Comparative Analysis* (New York: St Martin's Press, 1993).

—— and Blechman, B.M., *Keeping the Peace: The United Nations in the Emerging World Order* (Washington, DC: Henry L. Stimson Center, March 1992).

Ellsberg, D., *The Theory and Practice of Blackmail* (Santa Monica, CA: Rand, 1968).

Evans, E., *Mastering Negotiations* (London: Thorogood, 1998).

Evans, G.J., *Cooperating for Peace: The Global Agenda for the 1990s and Beyond* (St Leonards, NSW: Allen & Unwin, 1993).

Fasold, R., *Sociolinguistics of Language* (Oxford: Basil Blackwell, 1994).

Fetherston, A.B., *Towards a Theory of United Nations Peace-keeping* (Basingstoke: Macmillan, 1994).

Fishel, J.T., *Civil Military Operations in the New World* (New York: Praeger, 1997).

Fisher, R., Kopelman, E., Schneider, A.K., *Beyond Machiavelli: Tools for Coping with Conflict* (Cambridge, MA: Harvard University Press, 1994).

Fisher, R. and Schneider, A.K. (eds), *Coping with International Conflict: A Systematic Approach to Influence in International Negotiation* (Englewood Cliffs, NJ: Prentice-Hall, 1997).

Fisher, R. and Ury, W., *Getting to Yes* (Boston, MA: Houghton Mifflin, 1981).

Forster, L.M., 'Peace Operations: Forging the Instruments and Keeping the Edge', student paper (Carlisle Barracks: US Army War College, 2 April 1993).

George, A., *Avoiding War: Problems of Crisis Management* (Boulder, CO: Westview Press, 1991).

George, A. (ed.), *The Limits of Coercive Diplomacy* (Boston, MA: Little, Brown, 1971).

Glenny, M., *The Fall of Yugoslavia: The Third Balkan War*, 3rd rev. edn (Harmondsworth: Penguin, 1996).

Gordenker, L. and Weiss, T.G. (eds), *Soldiers, Peacekeepers and Disasters* (Basingstoke: Macmillan, 1991).

Groom, A.J.R., 'Problem-Solving in International Relations', in E.E. Azar and J.W. Burton, *International Conflict Resolution: Theory and Practice* (Brighton: Harvester/Wheatsheaf, 1986).

Guirdhan, M., *Communicating across Cultures* (Basingstoke: Macmillan, 1999).

Gulliver, P., *Disputes and Negotiations: A Cross-cultural Perspective* (New York: Academic Press, 1979).

Hargie, O., Saunders, C. and Dickson, D., *Social Skills in Interpersonal Communication* (London: Routledge, 1994).

Hathaway W., 'A New Way of Viewing Dispute Resolution Training', *Mediation Quarterly*, 13 (Fall 1995), pp. 37–45.

Heeler, F. (ed.), *Decision-making and Leadership* (Cambridge: Cambridge University Press, 1992).

Henderson, N., *Mandarin* (London: Weidenfeld & Nicolson, 1994).

Hill, S. and Malik, S.P. (eds), *Peacekeeping and the United Nations* (Aldershot: Dartmouth, 1996).

Holbrooke, R., *To End a War* (New York: Random House, 1998).

Holmes, R.L., *On War and Morality* (Princeton, NJ: Princeton University Press, 1989).

Holmes, W.M., 'The United Nations: Towards Being an Effective World Policeman', student paper (Carlisle Barracks: US Army War College, 1993).

Homans, G.C., *Social Behaviour* (New York: Harcourt Brace Jovanovich, 1961).

Honig, J.W. and Both, N., *Srebenica: Record of a War Crime* (Harmondsworth: Penguin, 1996).

Hooper, A. and Potter, J., *The Business of Leadership: Adding Lasting Value to your Organisation* (Aldershot: Ashgate, 1997).

Husim, S.B., *At War without Weapons* (North Branch, MN: Airlife, 1998).

Iklé, F.C., *How Nations Negotiate* (New York: Harper & Row, 1964).

International Peace Academy, *Peacekeeper's Handbook* (Oxford: Pergamon Press, 1984).

James, A., *The Politics of Peacekeeping* (London: Chatto & Windus, 1969).

Janowitz, M. and van Doorn, J., *On Military Ideology* (Rotterdam: Rotterdam University Press, 1971).

Johnson-Laird, P.N., *Mental Models* (Cambridge, MA: Harvard University Press, 1983).

Jones, E.E., 'The Rocky Road from Acts to Dispositions', *American Psychologist*, 34 (1979), pp. 107–17.

Kaplan, R., *Balkan Ghosts: A Journey through History* (New York: Vintage Books, 1993).

Kasper, G. and Kellerman, E., *Communication Strategies* (Harlow: Addison Wesley Longman, 1997).

Kegley, C.W., *Controversies in International Relations Theory: Realism and the Neoliberal Challenge* (Basingstoke: Macmillan, 1995).

Kissenger, H., *Diplomacy* (New York: Simon & Schuster, 1994).

Kremenyuk, V.A. (ed.), *International Negotiation: Analysis, Approaches, Issues* (San Francisco, CA: Jossey-Bass, 1991).

Lall, A., *Modern International Negotiations* (New York: Columbia University Press, 1966).

Lax, D.A. and Sebenius, J.K., *The Manager as Negotiator* (New York: Free Press, 1986).

Lewicki, R.J. (ed.), *Essentials of Negotiation* (New York: Irwin/McGraw-Hill, 1997).

Lockhart, C., *Bargaining in International Conflicts* (New York: Columbia University Press, 1989).

Maas, P., *Love Thy Neighbour: A Story of War* (New York: Vintage Books, 1997).

MacKenzie, L., *Peacekeeper* (Toronto: HarperCollins, 1993).

Mackinlay, J.A., *Guide to Peace Support Operations* (Providence, RI: Thomas J. Watson Jnr Institute for International Studies, 1996).

March, J.G. and Weissinger-Baylon, R., *Ambiguity and Command* (London: Pitman, 1986).

McRae, B., *Negotiating and Influencing Skills: The Art of Creating and Claiming Value* (New York: Sage, 1998).

Miall, H., *The Peacemakers: Peaceful Settlement of Disputes since 1945* (Basingstoke: Macmillan, 1992).

Morrison, A. (ed.), 'Canada: The Seasoned Veteran', draft paper prepared for the 35th annual convention of the International Studies Association, 28 March–1 April 1994, Washington DC.

Morrison, A., Fraser, D.A., Kiras, J.D. (eds), *Peacekeeping with Muscle: The Use of Force in International Conflict Resolution* (Toronto: Canadian Peacekeeping Press, 1997).

Moskos, C.C., *Peace Soldiers: The Sociology of a United Nations Military Force* (Chicago, IL: Chicago University Press, 1976).

Moyse, R. and Elsom-Cook, M.T., *Knowledge Negotiation* (London: Academic Press, 1992).

Neale, M.A. and Bazerman, M.H., *Cognition and Rationality in Negotiation* (New York: Free Press, 1991).

Negotiation Journal, 'On the Process of Dispute Settlement', 13: 1, 2, 3, 4 (1997).

Nierenberg, G.I., *The Art of Negotiating* (New York: Barnes & Noble, 1968).

Office of Legal Affairs, *Handbook on the Peaceful Settlement of Disputes between States* (New York: United Nations, 1992).

Peacekeepers' Handbook (Oxford: Pergamon Press, 1984).

Pruitt, D.G. and Carnevale, P.J., *Negotiation in Social Conflict* (Pacific Grove, CA: Brooks-Cole, 1993).

Raiffa, H., *Lectures on Negotiation Analysis* (Cambridge, MA: PON Books, 1996).

Rapoport, A., *Fights, Games and Debates* (Ann Arbor, MI: University of Michigan Press, 1960).

——, *Two-person Game Theory* (Ann Arbor, MI: University of Michigan Press, 1966).

Rikhye, I. and Skjelsbaek, J., *The United Nations and Peacekeeping: Results, Limitations and Prospects* (Basingstoke: Macmillan, 1990).

Roberts, A., *Humanitarian Action in War: Aid, Protection and Impartiality in a Policy Vacuum*, Adelphi Paper 305 (Oxford: Oxford University Press, 1996).

Rogan, S., Randell, G., Hammer, S., Mitchell, R., van Zandt, S., Clinton, R. (eds), *Dynamic Processes of Crisis Negotiation: Theory, Research and Practice* (New York: Praeger, 1997).

Rose, General Sir Michael, *Fighting for Peace* (London: Collins/Harvill, 1998).

Rosenau, J.N., *Turbulence in World Politics: A Theory of Change and Continuity* (Princeton, NJ: Princeton University Press, 1990).

Rothman, J., *From Confrontation to Cooperation: Resolving Ethnic and Regional Conflict* (New York: Sage, 1992).

Rouse, J. (ed.), 'On Looking into the Black Box: Prospects and Limits in the Search for Mental Models', in *Psychological Bulletin*, 100 (1986), pp. 359–63.

Rubin, J. and Brown, B., *The Social Psychology of Bargaining and Negotiation* (New York: Academic Press, 1975).

Schelling, T.C., *The Strategy of Conflict* (Cambridge, MA: Harvard University Press, 1960).

——, *Arms and Influence* (New York: Colonial Press, 1966).

Silber, L. and Little, A., *Yugoslavia: Death of a Nation*, rev. edn (Harmondsworth: Penguin, 1997).

Sivard, R.L., *World Military and Social Expenditures* (Leesburg, VA: World Priorities, SIPRI annual report 1985).

Smith, A.D., 'Conflict and Collective Identity: Class, Ethnie and Nation', in E.E. Azar and J.W. Burton (eds), *International Conflict Resolution: Theory and Practice* (Brighton: Harvester/Wheatsheaf, 1986).

Smith, J.D.D., *Canada in Croatia: Peacekeeping and UN Reform – the View from the Ground* (London: HMSO, 1995).

Steans, J., *Gender and International Relations* (Cambridge: Polity Press, 1998).

Steele, P., Murphy, J., Russill, R. (eds), *It's a Deal* (Maidenhead: McGraw-Hill, 1989).

Stevens, C.C., *Strategy and Collective Bargaining* (Maidenhead: McGraw-Hill, 1963).

The Blue Helmets: A Review of United Nations Peacekeeping (New York: United Nations, 1996).

Thompson, L., *The Mind and Heart of the Negotiator* (Englewood Cliffs, NJ: Prentice-Hall, 1998).

United Nations, *Disarmament and Conflict-Resolution Project: Managing*

Arms in Peace Processes: Aspects of Psychological Operations and Intelligence (New York and Geneva: UNIDIR, 1996).

Urquhart, B., *A Life in Peace and War* (New York: Harper & Row, 1987).

van Doorn, J., *On Military Ideology* (Rotterdam: Rotterdam University Press, 1971).

Walton, R.E. and McKersie, R.B., *A Behavioral Theory of Labor Negotiations* (New York: McGraw-Hill, 1965).

White, *Fearful Warriors: A Psychological Profile of US–Soviet Relations* (New York: Free Press, 1984).

Whittaker, D.J., *United Nations in Action* (London: University College Press, 1995).

——, *United Nations in the Contemporary World* (London: Routledge, 1997).

Woodcock, A. and Davis, D., *Analysis for Peace Operations* (Clementsport, Nova Scotia: Canadian Peacekeeping Press, 1998).

Wyler, R.S., 'The Prediction of Behaviour in Two-person Games', *Journal of Experimental Social Psychology* (November 1969), pp. 222–38.

Young, O., *The Politics of Force* (Princeton, NJ: Princeton University Press, 1968).

——, (ed.), *Bargaining* (Urbana, IL: Illinois University Press, 1975).

Index

Index